Chatham House Report

Xenia Dormandy with Rory Kinane
April 2014

G000114548

Asia-Pacific Security
A Changing Role for the United States

CHATHAM HOUSE
The Royal Institute of
International Affairs

Chatham House has been the home of the Royal Institute of International Affairs for more than ninety years. Our mission is to be a world-leading source of independent analysis, informed debate and influential ideas on how to build a prosperous and secure world for all.

The Royal Institute of International Affairs

Chatham House
10 St James's Square
London SW1Y 4LE
T: +44 (0) 20 7957 5700
F: + 44 (0) 20 7957 5710
www.chathamhouse.org

Charity Registration No. 208223

ISBN 978 1 78413 009 1

A catalogue record for this title is available from the British Library.

Cover image © Getty Images

Typeset by Soapbox, www.soapbox.co.uk

Printed and bound in Great Britain by Latimer Trend and Co Ltd

The material selected for the printing of this report is manufactured from 100% genuine de-inked post-consumer waste by an ISO 14001 certified mill and is Process Chlorine Free.

Contents

About the Authors

Xenia Dormandy is the Project Director of the US Programme and the Acting Dean of the Academy for Leadership in International Affairs at Chatham House. From 2009 to 2011, she was the Executive Director of the PeaceNexus Foundation in Switzerland. Prior to this, she was Executive Director of Harvard Kennedy School's Belfer Center for Science and International Affairs, Director of the Project on India and the Subcontinent, and a member of the Board of the Belfer Center. From 2001 to 2005, she worked in the US government, including at the State Department on issues ranging from non-proliferation to homeland security and South Asia. She also helped to set up the Homeland Security Office in the Office of the Vice President, and was Director for South Asia at the National Security Council.

She studied at Oxford University and received a Master's degree at Harvard University's Kennedy School. She is the author of numerous articles and op-eds, as well as the reports for Chatham House: *Prepared for Future Threats? US Defence Partnerships in the Asia-Pacific Region* and *The Next Chapter: President Obama's Second-Term Foreign Policy*.

Rory Kinane coordinates the US Programme at Chatham House. He has worked previously in parliamentary monitoring with DeHavilland Political Intelligence. In 2010, he won a place on the English Speaking Union's Parliamentary Exchange Programme and spent the summer in Washington, DC working for Congressman Brian Baird.

He received a Distinction for his Master's in International Relations from the University of Warwick where his focus was on US foreign policy and the CIA. In 2011–12 he was a volunteer Special Constable with the Metropolitan Police in Haringey, London. He also previously worked in the office of Andrew Dismore MP (former chair of the Joint Committee on Human Rights).

Acknowledgments

The research for and organization of this report benefited greatly from the assistance of the following people: Jennifer Leong, Richard Gowing, Stephanie Popp, Vishal Jalota, Kathleen McInnis, Glada Lahn, Jaakko Kooroshy, Antony Froggatt, Felix Preston, Dave Clemente, Kerry Brown, Allan Gyngell, Bates Gill, Lord Williams of Baglan, Nicolas Bouchet, Margaret May, Jing Huang, Kishore Mahbubani, and other individuals who assisted us from the Lee Kwan Yew School.

We would in particular like to thank the MacArthur Foundation, which generously supported this research project.

About the US Programme

The US Programme at Chatham House in London provides analysis on the changing role of America in the world. Building on the independent, international reputation of Chatham House, the programme provides a unique external perspective on the United States. The programme aims to:

- develop a contextual understanding of the transformations taking place within the US and internationally, to analyse how they affect US foreign policy;

- offer predictions on America's likely future international direction;

- influence responses from allies and others towards the US;

- highlight to American policy-makers the intended, and unintended, impact of their policies overseas.

The programme comprises both in-house staff and an international network of Associate Fellows who together provide in-depth expertise in both geographical and thematic areas.

About the MacArthur Foundation

The MacArthur Foundation supports creative people and effective institutions committed to building a more just, verdant, and peaceful world. In addition to selecting the MacArthur Fellows, the Foundation works to defend human rights, advance global conservation and security, make cities better places, and understand how technology is affecting children and society. More information is at www.macfound.org.

Acronyms and Abbreviations

AA/AD	Anti-Access/Area Denial
ADIZ	Air defence identification zone
ADMM	ASEAN Defence Ministers' Meeting
ADMM+	ASEAN Defence Ministers' Meeting Plus
APEC	Asia-Pacific Economic Cooperation
ARF	ASEAN Regional Forum
ASEAN	Association of Southeast Asian Nations
ASEAN+1	ASEAN+ another nation (typically China but can be India, the United States and others)
ASEAN+3	ASEAN+ Japan, China, South Korea
BIMSTEC	Bay of Bengal Initiative for Multi-Sectoral Technical and Economic Cooperation
BRICS	Brazil, Russia, India, China and South Africa
EAS	East Asia Summit
FTA	Free trade agreement
HADR	Humanitarian Assistance/Disaster Relief
NAM	Non-Aligned Movement
SAARC	South Asian Association for Regional Cooperation
SCO	Shanghai Cooperation Organization
TPP	Trans-Pacific Partnership

Executive Summary and Recommendations

America's role in the world is evolving. In part this is due to domestic factors such as rising economic constraints, a desire for 'nation-building at home', and war-weariness on the part of the public. But perhaps more profoundly, it results from changes in the broader international context and the types of external challenges the country faces. The range of policy instruments needed to respond to increasingly complex regional and global threats is also diversifying. At the same time, in contrast to the perception of the rise of new emerging economies (such as China, india and Brazil), in many parts of the world, including Asia, perceptions of the United States are that its power and leverage are in decline.

The United States has long maintained its leadership in the Asia-Pacific region. President Barack Obama made clear that America has every intention of continuing to sustain its leading role in this part of the world with the announcement in November 2011 of the 'rebalancing' (or 'pivot') of its foreign policy to Asia. However, what is less clear is how America's allies in the Asia-Pacific region see their own security interests changing and, given this, how they see the United States fitting into this new security framework. It is vital that both the demand for security (from Asia) and its supply (by the United States) are better understood in order to achieve a new status quo that meets the needs of all the players.

In 2012, a report entitled *Prepared for Future Threats? US Defence Partnerships in the Asia-Pacific Region*, also published by Chatham House, looked at whether the United States had the necessary relationships in the region to meet future challenges. This follow-up report considers six US allies or partners in Asia (Australia, India, Indonesia, Japan, Singapore and South Korea) and asks how they perceive their security interests and emerging threats – and, consequently, how they are addressing them through domestic capabilities and regional or plurilateral groups, and what role this suggests for the United States.

The principal findings are as follows.

The current situation

- The six Asia-Pacific states considered in this report have a broadly similar assessment of the range of perceived threats to their security. These include traditional ones – conflict with China, a North Korean collapse or attack, terrorism and insurgency – and non-traditional ones – natural-resource limitations (for example, food, water, oil and gas), attacks in cyberspace or on military or communications satellites, and economic vulnerabilities. However, there are significant variations and nuances in the size and nature of the threats, and how they are prioritized in each of these states.

- Current Asian institutions – the Association of Southeast Asian Nations (ASEAN), the East Asia Summit (EAS), Asia-Pacific Economic Cooperation (APEC) and others – are principally designed as venues for discussion. Their Asian members for the main part have no apparent desire for more active or action-oriented organizations. Asian leaders strongly value and endorse the current limited roles and functions of these entities. Western states, by contrast, often express a hope for more tangible outputs from them.

- Domestic and external perceptions of America's role in the world are changing. Despite President Obama's announcement of the US strategic rebalancing towards Asia, America's friends and allies are increasingly less confident of what position it will take in the region. Many of its regional allies and partners perceive it as becoming a less reliable partner (although one that is still far more reliable than others such as China). Each of its partners would like to see a slightly different role for the United States in the region, and thus there is no consensus position among them on this point.

The future

- As elsewhere, America's role in Asia will continue to change. Despite the rebalancing, cuts in US defence spending and greater political attention to domestic priorities are likely to lead to a less militarily assertive role in the region and perhaps, in time, a smaller permanent military presence there (possibly with more rotational troops, as is currently being seen in Japan and Australia). This will be partly compensated by ongoing improvements in US capabilities. The United States will, however, remain an Asia-Pacific power, and its continued focus should not be underestimated. Greater diplomatic resources are likely to be devoted to the region, and economic engagement (whether through trade agreements or development funds) is also likely to continue unabated or even increase over time.

- Over the next 15 years, non-traditional threats, whether natural or man-made, are likely to become more significant. Traditional state-driven conflicts are likely to play out initially in non-traditional ways, such as by constraining an adversary's economy or its access to natural resources, and through attacks in cyberspace or against military or communications satellites. Only as conflicts escalate will more traditional means be engaged, such as air, maritime and, finally, ground forces. Non-state actors, such as terrorists or insurgent groups, are also likely to employ such non-traditional levers where their capabilities allow.

- The severity of the impacts of natural, rather than man-made disasters is also likely to increase. Demand for oil, gas, water and food is rising exponentially across the region and expanding consumption is, in many cases, creating a new vicious cycle of resource stress. Military force is unlikely to play a leading role in alleviating these tensions.

- With rising defence expenditure, the six countries examined in this study are enhancing their traditional military capabilities. However, this alone will not be sufficient to protect them against the complex array of future threats. Other assets will be needed, including greater diplomatic resources to manage interlocking relations with regional allies and partners, and the diversification of economic and trading links to minimize each country's vulnerability to the actions of any other single actor, principally China.

- The Asia-Pacific states are already building up their informal alliances and partnerships with one another and with other states. The number and the depth of these informal relationships are likely to endure, and they will play an important role in maintaining stability in the region. Where they are between countries with similar interests (as between the United States, Japan and India), such plurilateral groups could eventually become the catalyst for more formal groupings focused on particular issues (e.g. combating piracy or terrorism). Where these link less aligned nations (as between China, Japan and South Korea) they are useful groups for discussion of potentially sensitive issues and building trust.

- While the proliferation of formal alliances with little or no operational authority has come under much criticism in the West, they form an expanding web that plays an important part in maintaining security in the region. By providing their traditional function as a talking shop for discussion of sensitive issues, they create a 'sponge' to defuse and, potentially, manage regional tensions. In addition, as natural threats become more prominent, given their less sensitive (and less zero-sum) nature, these groups might find a new more active role in addressing the resulting challenges. Building cooperation and collaboration in these forums, could, in time, create a framework for resolving more traditional areas of conflict.

- America will continue to play a central role in the region for some time to come, but not indefinitely as the lead actor. It will be looking in Asia, as elsewhere, to share the burdens of leadership. In the next 15 years, Asians may well have to get used to a situation with which Europeans are only just coming to terms – a United States that is a very important regional actor, but not always the first or principal port of call for ensuring security.

1. Introduction

The Second World War confirmed the United States as a major Asia-Pacific power. Many countries in the region depend on its conventional military power, diplomatic influence and nuclear umbrella in order to meet their security needs. But much has changed in the past 60 years and the pace of transformation is accelerating. The economies of China and India are growing rapidly, overall US defence spending is decreasing, and countries in the region are re-examining their national security and foreign policies. Some argue that the Asia-Pacific region is not only one of the most unstable areas of the world today but that it is becoming more so.[1]

It is against this backdrop that President Barack Obama announced the US 'pivot' (later rebranded 'rebalancing') to Asia in November 2011. A number of initiatives followed. These have included plans to rotate 2,500 marines into Darwin, Australia, the positioning of two littoral ships in Singapore, sending an additional 800 troops to South Korea, and increasing the scope and depth of defence engagement with countries such as Vietnam, the Philippines, Australia, Singapore and India.[2] All of this was done with an eye towards continued regional involvement in the future. The United States has stated that it plans to focus a greater proportion of its resources on Asia.[3]

As the United States has expanded and solidified its bilateral links in the region, it has also tried to promote closer ties between its allies and partners in areas of common interest. Through the Association of Southeast Asian Nations (ASEAN), countries in the region have convened expert working groups on a variety of defence issues (including, but not limited to, peacekeeping and de-mining) and have conducted humanitarian assistance/disaster relief (HADR) multilateral military exercises.[4] The United States continues to emphasize the importance of the Six-Party Talks with North Korea (despite the fact that they have been effectively on hold for six years). It has also worked diplomatically to bring friends together informally.

On the whole, the US security objective in the region has been fairly transparent: to build stronger bilateral and multilateral networks of allies and partners. This approach was expressed succinctly in a 2013 speech by National Security Advisor Tom Donilon, when he argued: 'For all of the changes in Asia, this much is settled: our alliances in the region have been and will remain the foundation of our strategy.'[5] By contrast, the objectives (and nuances) of America's principal partners are far less well understood, and particularly by American policy-makers. Most countries in the region have for many years started from the position of how they can work more effectively with the United States before considering other approaches to enhancing their security.

> **On the whole, the US security objective in the region has been fairly transparent: to build stronger bilateral and multilateral networks of allies and partners.**

Perhaps owing to their exclusive focus on their bilateral relationships with the United States, friends and allies appear to have been both reassured and discouraged in almost equal measure by the 'pivot'.[6] The perceived focus on security made some in the Asia-Pacific region nervous that China would find the US moves unduly antagonistic, concerns that have not been alleviated by official statements emphasizing the diplomatic and economic aspects of the 'pivot'. Yet, almost paradoxically, many are questioning whether the United States is really willing to adhere to its security obligations in the Pacific. Secretary of State John Kerry's remarks in Tokyo on 14 April 2013 regarding the Senkaku/Diaoyu Islands illustrates how the disparity between the rebalancing and more recent rhetoric appears particularly stark to America's allies.[7] The United States is trying to balance between reinforcing its allies while also dissuading them from taking aggressive actions and deterring potential adversaries.

Challenges in the Asia-Pacific region

The assumption that the United States will be willing and able to address robustly the security concerns of its allies in the Asia-Pacific region is increasingly under scrutiny. Fiscal pressures induced by the 2008 recession are forcing it to curtail its defence budget. Since 2011, the United States has announced around $1 trillion of defence cuts over the

---

[1] Council on Foreign Relations, 'Preventive Priorities Survey: 2013', 20 December 2012, http://www.cfr.org/conflict-prevention/preventive-priorities-survey-2013/p29673.
[2] 'United States sending more troops and tanks to South Korea', Reuters, 7 January 2014, http://www.reuters.com/article/2014/01/08/us-korea-usa-troops-idUSBREA061AU20140108.
[3] 'Leon Panetta: US to deploy 60% of navy fleet to Pacific', BBC News, 12 June 2012, http://www.bbc.co.uk/news/world-us-canada-18305750.
[4] Martin Sieff, 'ASEAN defense ministers host disaster relief, military medicine exercise', *Asia Pacific Defense Forum*, 28 June 2013, http://apdforum.com/en_GB/article/rmiap/articles/online/features/2013/06/28/asean-disaster-relief.
[5] Tom Donilon, 'The United States and the Asia-Pacific in 2013', Remarks to the Asia Society, 11 March 2013, http://www.whitehouse.gov/the-press-office/2013/03/11/remarks-tom-donilon-national-security-advisory-president-united-states-a.
[6] Formal allies to the United States in Asia-Pacific include Japan, the Philippines, Australia, New Zealand, South Korea and Thailand.
[7] John Kerry, 'Joint Press Availability With Japanese Foreign Minister Kishida After Their Meeting', 14 April 2013, http://www.state.gov/secretary/remarks/2013/04/207483.htm. See page 11 below for fuller details of this incident.

coming decade (the annual defence budget stands at $600 billion).[8] So while it is increasing its presence in Asia, its global footprint is shrinking: Asia's slice is getting bigger, but the pie is getting smaller. Over time, it is likely that America's allies and friends will need to compensate for the diminution of US assets in the region.

Furthermore, America's allies will need to do so in the face of increased Chinese military spending and activism. China has budgeted a 12.2% increase in defence spending in 2014, continuing a trend of nearly two decades of double-digit growth. Together with the US cuts, this prompted many to question whether the balance of power between the United States and China is shifting.[9] Furthermore, since 2010, China has been flexing its military muscle, leading in 2011 to heightened tensions with the Philippines over the Scarborough Shoal, and in 2012 and 2013 to tensions with Japan over the Senkaku/Diaoyu Islands. In July 2013, China and Russia held joint naval exercises close to Japan, which has, in recent years, notably strengthened its coastguard capabilities.[10] At the same time, China is the strongest trading partner for many of the countries concerned. A 2009 study found that, while most publics surveyed in the region expected China to be the most important regional power in the near future, they also overwhelmingly trusted the United States more.[11] Regardless, oft-quoted perceptions of US decline and Chinese rise have significant policy implications for countries and how they manage their relationships with these two big powers.

Over the past year or so, there have also been leadership changes in a number of the major regional powers. In November 2012, the handover of Chinese leadership commenced, and President Xi Jinping took office at the National People's Congress in March 2013. However, what kind of foreign policy he will pursue is still in question. In December 2012, Shinzo Abe was re-elected prime minister of Japan, just over five years after he last held the office.[12] In February 2013, Park Geun-hye became president of South Korea, bringing, among other things, a new tougher policy on North Korea and a harder nationalistic line on Japan. And in September 2013, Australia elected a new leader, Tony Abbott. Thus four of the region's major powers have experienced a transfer of leadership that has produced what many would describe as a more nationalistic government.

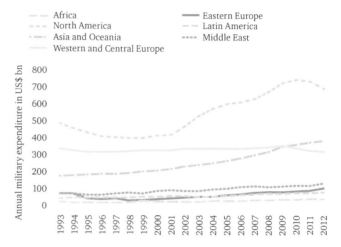

Figure 1: Regional defence spending

Source: Stockholm International Peace Research Institute (SIPRI), Military Expenditure Database, http://www.sipri.org/research/armaments/milex/milex_database/milex_database.

Changing international security dynamics

The nature of the international strategic environment is also changing. As the US National Intelligence Council *Global Trends 2030* report and a European Union Institute for Security Studies report have argued, increased global interconnectivity means individuals now are empowered as never before, while non-state actors can make an unprecedentedly significant strategic impact.[13] While traditional threats certainly still exist, emerging challenges such as cyber security, transnational terrorism, and food and water scarcity are becoming increasingly prominent items on many Asian countries' security agendas.

These dynamics are likely to become exponentially more complex. New technologies will empower more actors. Faster communications will make it necessary for states to respond more quickly before events escalate. And yet governments still often move bureaucratically and slowly. Given tight budgets, it is hard for states to look towards and prepare for possible challenges 10 or 15 years in the future that feel less tangible than those currently being faced. Yet the defence industry demands such forward thinking in

---

[8] International Institute for Strategic Studies (IISS), *The Military Balance 2014* (London: Routledge 2014).

[9] 'China Boosts Defense Spending as Military Modernizes Arsenal', Bloomberg News, 5 March 2013, http://www.bloomberg.com/news/2013-03-05/china-boosts-defense-spending-as-military-modernizes-its-arsenal.html; and Carnegie Endowment for International Peace, 'China's Military and the US-Japan Alliance in 2030: A Strategic Net Assessment', 3 May 2013, http://carnegieendowment.org/2013/05/03/china-s-military-and-US-japan-alliance-in-2030-strategic-net-assessment/g1wh.

[10] Tiago Mauricio, 'PacNet #60 – Abenomics and Japan's Defense Priorities', Centre for Strategic and International Studies, 5 August 2013, https://csis.org/publication/pacnet-60-abenomics-and-japans-defense-priorities.

[11] Bates Gill et al., 'Strategic Views on Asian Nationalism', Centre for Strategic and International Studies, February 2009, http://csis.org/files/media/csis/pubs/090217_gill_stratviews_web.pdf, p. 5.

[12] Prime Minister Abe served less than a year in his first term in office, from 26 September 2006 to 12 September 2007.

[13] European Union Institute for Security Studies, 'Global Trends 2030: Citizens in an Interconnected and Polycentric World', October 2011, http://www.iss.europa.eu/uploads/media/ESPAS_report_01.pdf.

order to ensure production capacity is maintained and new research and development is invested in the right areas. Given its ongoing tensions and dynamism, nowhere is foresight and strategic planning more vital than in the Asia-Pacific region.

It is in this context that this report examines the security interests of a number of Asia-Pacific powers – Australia, India, Indonesia, Japan, Singapore and South Korea – that are friends or allies of the United States. (While India is not an Asia-Pacific state it is included here as a significant power in the region.) This study explores their interests, the threats to those interests, and how they are responding to these threats internally, with regard to their regional relationships and with respect to a changing role for the United States. Understanding the interests of these major regional players is the first step towards enhancing the transparency that is needed in order to build more effective and open relationships and networks.

2. Background

This chapter provides a brief background on the positions of Australia, India, Indonesia, Japan, Singapore and South Korea, as well as of the major regional groupings. The capabilities of each, the details of their relationship with the United States and their most important regional relationships are outlined.[14]

Australia

Military budget 2013: $26bn

Military budget as a percentage of GDP: 1.6%

Active forces: 56,200 (Army 28,600; Navy 13,550; Air Force 14,050; Reserves 28,550)

Australia faces a very different set of challenges from those confronting the other countries in this study. Given its geographic remoteness and unique history in the region as a Western-orientated power, it is largely divorced from (but keenly aware of) the historical and contemporary conflicts between countries to its north. Despite its large landmass, it has a relatively small population (22 million) and is reliant on working with others to maintain its security. It is highly dependent on open sea lanes and recognizes its vulnerability to threats in the maritime and air arena, and its inability to meet those threats alone.

Since coming to office in September 2013, Prime Minister Tony Abbott has made clear he wants to focus more on local relations and less on multilateral institutions than his predecessor, Kevin Rudd (an oft-quoted statement during the election campaign was 'more Jakarta, less Geneva').[15] Many Australians are sceptical of the efficacy of multilateral institutions in managing regional security dynamics. However, it is unlikely that Australian foreign policy will take a major turn and there is a strong bipartisan agreement regarding the core principle of foreign and defence policy: namely, strengthening the bilateral relationship with the United States.

Regional relationships

China presents the most difficult balancing act for Australian relations. As for many other countries in the region, it is Australia's largest trading partner, accounting for $115 billion a year.[16] In the second quarter of 2013, it accounted for 35.4% of Australian exports, including a large amount of natural resources, manufactured goods and agricultural products.[17] However, conscious of not wanting to develop too strong a dependency on the regional giant, Australia has been working to expand its economic links with other regional partners such as India. On the other hand, Australia does not have a strong investment relationship with China (except increasingly in the case of the minerals-rich state of Western Australia). Its biggest investment partner by far is the United States.[18]

Abbott suggested during the election campaign that in office he would promote Australia's bilateral relationship with India, stressing that the two countries 'have much more common in terms of values and interests than most other countries in this region'.[19] Nevertheless, it is too early to tell yet whether he will make a significant change to the approach that was fostered under the previous government.

Australia has also increased engagement with ASEAN and Japan on defence.[20] In September 2012, Japan and Australia pledged to work more closely on defence issues and declared each other 'natural strategic partners'.[21] In October 2013, Abbott stated that 'Japan is Australia's best friend in Asia and we want to keep it a very strong friendship'.[22] The two countries share a strong desire to ensure open sea lanes and to maintain the US presence in the region. In different ways, both view the growth of China with concern. Since 2002, they have participated in a formal trilateral dialogue with the United States (which the latter is looking to strengthen).[23]

Relations with Indonesia have developed significantly from a low point in 1999 when Australia supported the breakaway aspirations of East Timor, calling for a referendum for self-determination and leading a multinational peacekeeping force there after an

---

[14] Except where otherwise stated, all military data in the boxes are derived from IISS, *The Military Balance 2014* (London: Routledge, 2014).

[15] Sam Bateman, 'PacNet #70 – Australia under Abbott: What It Means for the Region', 10 September 2013, http://csis.org/files/publication/Pac1370.pdf.

[16] Pam Walker, 'Does Tony Abbott get China? Challenge for next Australian leader', *South China Morning Post*, 6 September 2013, http://www.scmp.com/news/asia/article/1304186/does-tony-abbott-get-china-challenge-next-australian-leader.

[17] Angus Grigg and Lisa Murray, 'Australia-China trade no longer just a resources story', *Financial Review*, 21 August 2013, http://www.afr.com/p/australia2-0/australia_china_trade_no_longer_BR858fGu3LCDM0n3NzUDhJ.

[18] New South Wales Government, Trade and Investment, 'Stock of Foreign Direct Investment in Australia by Country as of 31 December 2011', http://www.business.nsw.gov.au/invest-in-nsw/about-nsw/trade-and-investment/stock-of-foreign-direct-investment-in-australia-by-country.

[19] 'India-Australia ties likely to get boost under PM-elect Tony Abbott', *Economic Times*, 10 September 2013, http://articles.economictimes.indiatimes.com/2013-09-10/news/41937892_1_indian-ocean-australia-india-institute-india-australia-ties.

[20] Australian Government, Department of Defense, 'Defense White Paper 2013', http://www.defence.gov.au/whitepaper2013/docs/WP_2013_web.pdf, p. 58.

[21] Hamish McDonald, 'Australia, Japan pledge closer defence ties', *Sydney Morning Herald*, 15 September 2012, http://www.smh.com.au/national/australia-japan-pledge-closer-defence-ties-2012,0914-25xmh.html.

[22] Naomi Woodley, 'Prime Minister Tony Abbott holds first formal meeting with Japanese PM Shinzo Abe', ABC News, 10 October 2013, http://www.abc.net.au/news/2013-10-09/tony-abbott-png-trade-china-economy-brunei/5012868.

[23] 'US-Japan-Australia: A Trilateral with Purpose?', *The Diplomat*, 25 October 2013, http://thediplomat.com/2013/10/u-s-japan-australia-a-trilateral-with-purpose/1/.

Map of the Asia-Pacific region

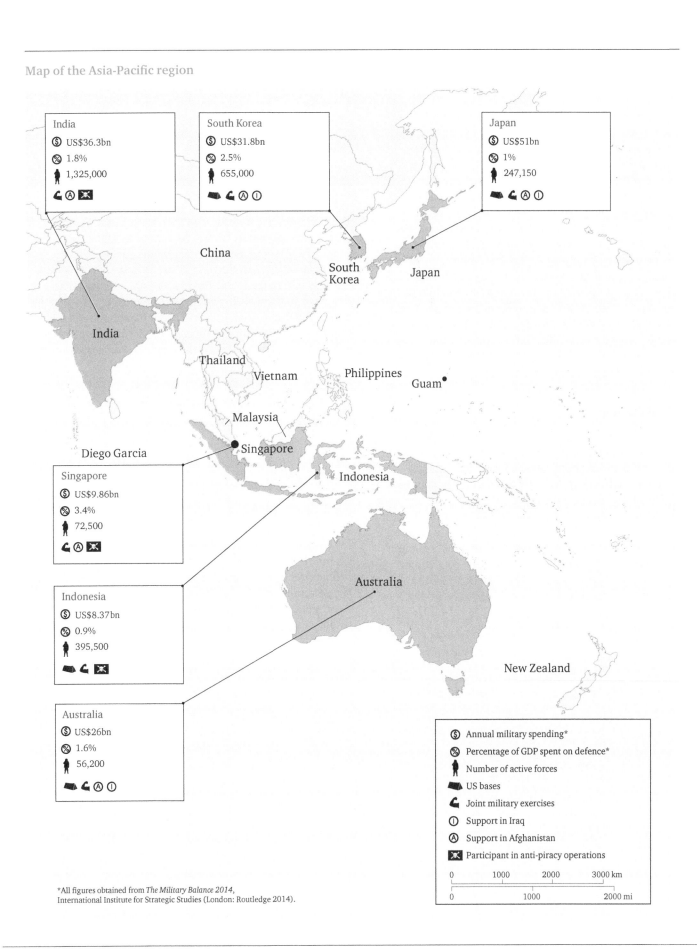

India
- ⑤ US$36.3bn
- ⑳ 1.8%
- 👤 1,325,000
- ⊂ Ⓐ ✖

South Korea
- ⑤ US$31.8bn
- ⑳ 2.5%
- 👤 655,000
- ◤ ⊂ Ⓐ ①

Japan
- ⑤ US$51bn
- ⑳ 1%
- 👤 247,150
- ◤ ⊂ Ⓐ ①

Singapore
- ⑤ US$9.86bn
- ⑳ 3.4%
- 👤 72,500
- ⊂ Ⓐ ✖

Indonesia
- ⑤ US$8.37bn
- ⑳ 0.9%
- 👤 395,500
- ◤ ⊂ ✖

Australia
- ⑤ US$26bn
- ⑳ 1.6%
- 👤 56,200
- ◤ ⊂ Ⓐ ①

China

South Korea

Japan

India

Thailand

Vietnam

Philippines

Guam

Malaysia

Diego Garcia

Singapore

Indonesia

Australia

New Zealand

Legend
- ⑤ Annual military spending*
- ⑳ Percentage of GDP spent on defence*
- 👤 Number of active forces
- ◤ US bases
- ⊂ Joint military exercises
- ① Support in Iraq
- Ⓐ Support in Afghanistan
- ✖ Participant in anti-piracy operations

| 0 | 1000 | 2000 | 3000 km |

| 0 | 1000 | 2000 mi |

*All figures obtained from *The Military Balance 2014*,
International Institute for Strategic Studies (London: Routledge 2014).

overwhelmingly pro-independence vote sparked violent protests.[24] Bilateral trade has increased substantially since 2000 (except during the SARS outbreak of 2002–03), with merchandise trade flows growing on average by 7.2% per year for over a decade.[25] From 2010/11 to 2011/12 total trade grew by 8.3% to $14.9 billion. Since 2007, there have been over 130 two-way ministerial visits and in 2010 the two countries elevated their relationship to the status of a 'comprehensive strategic partnership'.[26] However, tensions remain on issues ranging from cattle trade to immigration.[27] In November 2013, Indonesia recalled its ambassador over revelations of Australian spying on President Susilo Bambang Yudhoyono.[28] It then suspended military cooperation on issues including combating people-smuggling, joint military exercises and intelligence exchange.[29] The ability of the two countries to overcome these challenges will be very dependent on who wins the Indonesian election in July 2014; President Yudhoyono has been very pro-Australian but it is not clear what will follow under his eventual successor.

US relationship

Australia is heavily dependent upon its relationship with the United States to underpin its overall security posture, and recognizes it as its key strategic ally. They fought alongside each other in the Second World War, and the strategic relationship is underpinned by the 1951 Australia, New Zealand and United States (ANZUS) Security Treaty, which places Australia under America's extended nuclear umbrella. The Second World War also saw the beginning of extensive Australian signals intelligence cooperation with the United States under the auspices of the 'Five Eyes' agreement (also involving the United Kingdom, New Zealand and Canada).[30]

In the context of its dependence on the United States for stability and maintaining open sea lanes Australia has been particularly happy with the pivot and largely welcomed the plan to rotate 2,500 US Marines into Darwin.[31] It has indicated a willingness to expand current cooperation agreements with the US military, such as granting access to airfields in its Northern Territory and the HMAS Stirling Naval Base in Western Australia.[32] It has also agreed to the establishment of American C-band space surveillance radar and the transfer of an advanced space surveillance telescope to Western Australia.[33]

This collaborative attitude also frames Australia's willingness to support US-led operations in Afghanistan, Iraq and elsewhere, recognizing that in order to get American buy-in in the region, it needs to share US security burdens too. Indeed, over the past decade, Australia has demonstrated increasing willingness not just to take part in, but to lead military coalitions in order to manage crises in the Asia-Pacific region. As such, Australia led interventions in East Timor, Papua New Guinea and the Solomon Islands.

> This collaborative attitude also frames Australia's willingness to support US-led operations in Afghanistan, Iraq and elsewhere, recognizing that in order to get American buy-in in the region, it needs to share US security burdens too.

Prime Minister Abbott has promised to raise defence expenditure to 2% of Australian GDP over the next 10 years (although it remains unclear how this will be achieved).[34] On the other hand, he has pledged to review 'big ticket' defence items, including participation in the US Joint Strike Fighter project.[35] Despite the completion of a Defence White Paper in 2013, he has also promised a new review in the coming years.[36]

[24] 'World: Asia-Pacific UN approves Timor force', BBC News, 15 September 1999, http://news.bbc.co.uk/1/hi/world/asia-pacific/447639.stm.

[25] Centre for International Economics, Canberra & Sydney, 'Estimating the impact of an Australia–Indonesia trade and investment agreement', Report prepared for the Department of Foreign Affairs and Trade, January 2009, http://www.dfat.gov.au/fta/iacepa/aus-indon_fta_cie.pdf.

[26] Australian Government, Department of Foreign Affairs, 'Indonesia country brief', January 2014, http://www.dfat.gov.au/geo/indonesia/indonesia_brief.html.

[27] Phil Mercer, 'Australia, Indonesia seek to repair strained relations; cattle deal reached', Voice of America, 2 October 2013, http://www.voanews.com/content/australia-indonesia-seek-to-repair-strained-relations-cattle-deal-reached/1761164.html.

[28] 'Indonesia leader says Australia spying damaged ties', BBC News, 19 November 2013, http://www.bbc.co.uk/news/world-asia-24986093.

[29] 'Indonesia halts Australia cooperation amid spying row', BBC News, 20 November 2013, http://www.bbc.co.uk/news/world-asia-25000545?utm_source=Sailthru&utm_medium=email&utm_term=*Morning%20Brief&utm_campaign=MB%2011,.20.13.

[30] 'History of 5-Eyes – explainer', The Guardian, 2 December 2013, http://www.theguardian.com/world/2013/dec/02/history-of-5-eyes-explainer.

[31] Seth Robson, 'US increasing number of Marines on rotation to Australia', Stars and Stripes, 14 June 2013, http://www.stripes.com/news/pacific/us-increasing-number-of-marines-on-rotation-to-australia-1.225843.

[32] Bates Gill, 'Alliances under Austerity: What does America want?', Strategic & Defence Studies Centre Discussion Paper, February 2013, http://ips.cap.anu.edu.au/publications/alliances-under-austerity-what-does-america-want.

[33] Ibid.

[34] Brendan Nicholson, 'US welcomes defence spending rise', The Australian, 12 September 2013, http://www.theaustralian.com.au/national-affairs/election-2013/us-welcomes-defence-spending-rise/story-fn9qr68y-1226717224082#.

[35] Bateman, 'PacNet #70 – Australia under Abbott'.

[36] James Brown and Rory Medcalf, 'Fleet review good start, now for Defence', The Australian, 27 October 2013, http://www.theaustralian.com.au/national-affairs/opinion/fleet-review-good-start-now-for-defence/story-e6frgd0x-1226733816122#.

India

Military budget 2013: $36.3bn

Military budget as a percentage of GDP: 1.8%

Active forces: 1,325,000 (Army 1,129,900; Navy 58,350; Air Force 127,200; Coast Guard 9,550; Reserves 1,155,000)

India is the world's largest democracy and on course to have its largest population (exceeding China's by around 2035). By some estimates it could also overtake China (which will itself by then have surpassed the United States) to become the largest economy in the world by 2048.[37] India sees itself with a burgeoning regional and global role. As this develops, it is moving away from its traditional stance as a leader of the Non-Aligned Movement (NAM). However, it still finds itself being pulled in different directions by its economic interests, its desire for global recognition and its historical NAM thinking. India views catching up with China as a key priority, even if that is a long-term goal.

Given its size and location outside the Asia-Pacific region, India is in a different strategic position from many of the other countries in this study, and is less likely to get drawn into a conflict not of its own making. Nevertheless, it is increasing its military capabilities and in 2013 purchased a third aircraft carrier.[38]

Despite its great potential, India is often criticized for lacking a strategic vision internationally and for failing to deal with its internal problems. While it wants to be more involved in the region, therefore, it could be argued that India is failing to take full advantage of the opportunity to become a more significant international actor.[39]

Regional relationships

Border disputes between India and China continue and, in response to a provocation in April 2013, India created a new army unit of 50,000 soldiers.[40] It also remains worried about Pakistan's relationship with China, for example over the latter's decision to help Pakistan produce at least 50 JF-17 jets.[41] India is inherently less vulnerable to Chinese pressure than many other regional powers, not least as China's economic growth is more susceptible to tensions with India. Their economies are tied to each other through a strong trade relationship (valued at up to $66.7 billion in the 2012/13 financial year), although concerns are mounting in India over the trade deficit between them.[42]

India's other major regional threat comes from Pakistan. Increasingly its concern is over the role of terrorist groups crossing the Line of Control in Kashmir rather than a direct interstate conflict. Relations have marginally improved since Nawaz Sharif became prime minister of Pakistan in 2013, as he had stated this as one of his early goals. However, with the upcoming elections in India, it is unclear how a new leadership will approach this challenge.

India has also engaged far more actively in recent years in closer trilateral relationships with the United States and a number of other Asia-Pacific states, including Australia and Japan. These dialogues are strong on strategic discussion but far less so on concrete collaboration; there remains much scope to improve cooperation in areas such as information exchange or military training.[43] Australia is expected to facilitate a number of new initiatives with India, such as supplying it with uranium, and ramping up several older ones, such as defence cooperation, vocational training, joint scientific research and water management.[44]

There remains great potential for India to increase cooperation and trade with ASEAN.[45] It aims to increase trade with the group from the current $80 billion to $200 billion by 2022.[46]

---

[37] Emma Rowley, 'India will become world's biggest economy in less than 40 years', *Daily Telegraph*, 16 July 2013, http://www.telegraph.co.uk/finance/economics/10182819/India-will-become-worlds-biggest-economy-in-less-than-40-years.html.

[38] Conal Urquhart, 'India buys third aircraft carrier amid rivalry with China', *The Guardian*, 16 November 2013, http://www.theguardian.com/world/2013/nov/16/india-aircraft-carrier-russia-rivalry-china.

[39] 'India as a great power: know your own strength', *The Economist*, 30 March 2013, http://www.economist.com/news/briefing/21574458-india-poised-become-one-four-largest-military-powers-world-end.

[40] In April 2013 30 Chinese soldiers camped on the Indian side of a disputed border area for three weeks. See Victor Mallet, 'India to add 50,000 troops to protect China border', *The Financial Times*, 18 July 2013, http://www.ft.com/cms/s/0/000a98d4-ef7d-11e2-a237-00144feabdc0.html#axzz2ZOK114Cs.

[41] Ibid.

[42] 'India's trade deficit with China balloons to $12 billion', *Times of India*, 1 July 2013, http://timesofindia.indiatimes.com/business/india-business/Indias-trade-deficit-with-China-balloons-to-12-billion/articleshow/20861239.cms.

[43] Sourabh Gupta, 'PacNet #39 – Japan-India Strategic Ties: Time to Move Beyond Mere Words', Centre for Strategic and International Studies, 6 June 2013, http://csis.org/files/publication/Pac1370.pdf.

[44] 'New Australian government flags better ties with India', *Authint Mail*, 19 October 2013, https://www.authintmail.com/article/opinion/new-australian-government-flags-better-ties-india.

[45] Ted Osius, 'Enhancing India-ASEAN Connectivity', Center for Strategic and International Studies, June 2013, http://csis.org/files/publication/130621_Osius_EnhancingIndiaASEAN_WEB.pdf.

[46] Ibid.

US relationship

Throughout the Cold War India's relationship with the United States was difficult, owing to India's prominent leadership of the NAM and, within that structure, its leaning towards the Soviet Union. In recent years, the relationship has improved greatly with the 2005 signing of the US–India Civil Nuclear Agreement, and a more recent defence agreement in 2013. President Obama has tried to add further momentum to the relationship, announcing US support for India's permanent membership of the UN Security Council (citing 'India's long history as a leading contributor to United Nations peacekeeping missions') and major efforts, led by then Deputy Secretary of Defense Ashton Carter, to promote more effective defence sales between the two countries.[47] There are hopes in the United States that the elections in April and May 2014 and a new leadership in India might revitalize the bilateral relationship and unstick a number of economic and other initiatives.

Secretary of Defense Chuck Hagel has made it clear he hopes to expand and improve the relationship further.[48] Arms sales to India have grown dramatically from a low base to over $8 billion today, and the United States hopes for a significant expansion in coming years, particularly as India intends to spend $100 billion over the next decade on improving its military hardware.[49] The two countries also engage regularly in joint military exercises and in other areas of collaboration, including non-proliferation, counter-terrorism and managing the global commons.

Indonesia

Military budget 2013: $8.37bn

Military budget as a percentage of GDP: 0.9%

Active forces: 395,500 (Army 300,400; Navy 65,000; Air Force 30,100; Reserves 400,000)

Indonesia, like India, was one of the founders of the Non-Aligned Movement and is now a growing regional power. Its leaders contrast their approach to regional-power status with that of India, suggesting that while the latter emphasizes its size and power, Indonesia takes a softer approach, focusing on collaboration with other countries in the region and downplaying its individual power. It explicitly rejects replicating what some saw as India's more assertive efforts at leading South Asia in the early 2000s.

Indonesia has retained its independent mindset, expressing strongly its intention not to define itself as balancing between the United States and China. As President Yudhoyono said in his second inaugural address in 2009, Indonesia considers itself to have 'a million friends and zero enemies' and is very focused on the idea of 'self-resilience'.[50] Attention is focused far more on internal security threats, particularly separatism, than the possibility of external threats. Indonesia spends relatively little on defence – 0.9% of GDP – although this is set to rise in the coming years.[51]

Regional relationships

Indonesia sees ASEAN as the cornerstone of its foreign policy and as a means to leverage power without antagonizing its neighbours. As the implicit leader in ASEAN, it would like the organization to take a more robust role, but it relies on consensus to achieve this. It is keen not to be seen as the head of ASEAN and as imposing its interests on others within the grouping. Indonesia also recognizes the relatively limited power of each ASEAN member alone and therefore values collaboration.

Indonesia has enhanced its engagement with Australia, as mentioned previously, but it was deeply perturbed by the November 2013 revelations of Australia's spying and by its efforts to drive back asylum-seekers, including entry by the Australian navy into Indonesian territorial waters.[52] Indonesia has some fears over China becoming a regional hegemon but feels less immediately threatened than some others in the region that have territorial disputes with China.[53] Trade between China and Indonesia has increased

---

[47] Colum Lynch, 'India threatens to pull plug on peacekeeping', *Foreign Policy*, 14 June 2011, http://blog.foreignpolicy.com/posts/2011,/06/14/india_threatens_to_pull_plug_on_peacekeeping.

[48] 'India-US defence ties made tremendous progress under Obama', Zee News, 6 September 2013, http://zeenews.india.com/news/nation/india-us-defence-ties-made-tremendous-progress-under-obama_874542.html.

[49] Andrea Shalal-Esa, 'US aims to expand India arms trade by "billions of dollars"', Reuters, 19 April 2013, http://in.reuters.com/article/2013/04/18/usa-india-weapons-idINDEE93H0F220130418.

[50] 'SBY: Indonesia has "a million friends and zero enemies"', *Jakarta Globe*, 20 October 2009 http://www.thejakartaglobe.com/archive/sby-indonesia-has-a-million-friends-and-zero-enemies/?doing_wp_cron=1393242839.9316298961639404296875.

[51] IISS, *The Military Balance 2014*, p. 488.

[52] 'Indonesia halts Australia cooperation amid spying row', BBC News, 20 November 2013, http://www.bbc.co.uk/news/world-asia-25000545?utm_source=Sailthru&utm_medium=email&utm_term=*Morning%20Brief&utm_campaign=MB%2011,.20.13; and Lenore Taylor, 'Australian vessels "unintentionally" entered Indonesian waters six times', *The Guardian*, 19 February 2014, http://www.theguardian.com/world/2014/feb/19/australian-vessels-unintentionally-entered-indonesian-waters-six-times.

[53] Daniel Bodirsky, 'US-Indonesian Relations: A Balancing Act', *Geopolitical Monitor*, 4 June 2012, http://www.geopoliticalmonitor.com/us-indonesian-relations-a-balancing-act-4684.

rapidly, following recent agreements, to almost $66.2 billion by 2012, with an agreement to increase bilateral trade to $80 billion by 2015.[54]

Indonesia maintains a close economic relationship with Japan, its trade being of roughly equal size to that with China.[55] A recent poll found Indonesia to be the most pro-Japanese country in the world, with 82% of those surveyed viewing Japan positively.[56]

US relationship

After a period during which military-to-military engagements were banned (as mandated in the United States by the Leahy Amendment that focused on human rights abuses by Indonesia's military), re-engagement began in 2010. Indonesia now hosts a small number of US troops and has participated in some joint military exercises, mainly focused on counter-terrorism. Following a 2010 visit by President Obama, military cooperation has increased; in 2011 the two countries held 140 joint military exercises.[57] In 2013, they held what was described as the 'largest and most complex bilateral event ever conducted between the US Army and Indonesia'.[58]

Indonesia wants the United States to act as a 'resident power' in the region, one that does not push an agenda but assists in maintaining stability. It remains largely supportive of the United States retaining its presence.

Japan

Military budget 2013: $51bn

Military budget as a percentage of GDP: 1%

Active forces: 247,150 (Ground 151,050; Maritime 45,500; Air Force 47,100; Central Staff 3,500; Paramilitary 12,650; Reserves 56,100)

In 2010, Japan was replaced by its long-time rival, China, as the largest economic power in Asia (and second largest globally). The psychological impact of this has compounded that which developed from two decades of slow growth, economic stagnation and national political stagnation. However, in recent months Prime Minister Shinzo Abe's government has restored some confidence in Japan through his 'three arrows' economic agenda and his announced review of the country's restrictive constitution to allow a more flexible interpretation of 'self-defence'.[59] Prime Minister Abe has stated his desire 'to make Japan's presence felt in the world'.[60] However, there are many dissenting views in Japan and much more needs to be done to solidify the planned economic and security reforms.

Under Abe, the country's 'dynamic defence' doctrine will remain central, with a strong focus on North Korea and China's more aggressive regional defence postures.[61] In January 2013, Japan raised defence spending for the first time in 11 years. Although the percentage rise seems modest by regional levels (0.8%),[62] it builds upon Japan's already advanced military, which has the fifth largest budget in the world.[63]

Japan remains a regional and global leader in many areas. Its importance is often overlooked in the US–Chinese bipolar narrative, but, given the size of its economy, its technological achievements and its military capabilities, it will continue to play an important role in a changing Asia.

Regional relationships

Japan is one of the largest trading countries in the region, with strong economic relationships with China, South Korea, Taiwan, Hong Kong, Indonesia and Australia. In 2008, China overtook the United States to become its largest trading partner.[64] Japan conducts over half its trade with Asia (and thus is very susceptible to economic upheaval in the region).

---

[54] 'China, Indonesia aim for 80 bln dollars in bilateral trade by 2015', Xinhuanet, 3 October 2013, http://news.xinhuanet.com/english/china/2013-10/03/c_132770911.htm.
[55] Indonesia Trade Forecast Report – HSBC Global Connections, HSBC, March 2014, https://globalconnections.hsbc.com/us/en/tools-data/trade-forecasts/id.
[56] 'Views of China and India slide while UK's ratings climb: global poll', BBC World Service, 22 May 2013, http://www.globescan.com/images/images/pressreleases/bbc2013_country_ratings/2013_country_rating_poll_bbc_globescan.pdf.
[57] 'US, Indonesia announce stepped up military cooperation', Voice of America, 24 July 2011, http://blogs.voanews.com/breaking-news/2011,/07/24/us-indonesia-announce-stepped-up-military-cooperation/.
[58] Bill Gertz, 'US, Indonesian forces conduct war games', *The Washington Free Beacon*, 18 July 2013, http://freebeacon.com/national-security/u-s-indonesian-forces-conduct-war-games/.
[59] For an explanation of the potential consequences of such a change, Noboru Yamaguchi, 'Japan's Changing Defence Policy', Meeting Summary, Chatham House, July 2013, http://www.chathamhouse.org/publications/papers/view/193923.
[60] Jonathan Soble, 'Abe issues party rallying cry after poll win', *Financial Times*, 22 July 2013, http://www.ft.com/cms/s/0/0df2dd28-f2b9-11e2-a203-00144feabdc0.html?siteedition=uk#axzz2uFWomgwq.
[61] John Swenson-Wright, *Is Japan Truly 'Back'? Prospects for a More Proactive Security Policy*, Briefing Paper, Chatham House, June 2013, http://www.chathamhouse.org/publications/papers/view/192477.
[62] Compared with a 33.3% rise in real terms in 2012 in Indonesia, 8.3% in China and 2.3% in Singapore. IISS, *The Military Balance 2013*.
[63] Liu Yunlong, 'Japan increases military expansion for next year', *Global Times*, December 26, 2013, http://www.globaltimes.cn/content/834200.shtml#.Uw4QYM4SrAp.
[64] Japan External Trade Organization, as of February 2013, http://www.jetro.go.jp/en/reports/statistics/.

According to Pew Research, Japan remains fairly popular across Asia despite its imperial legacy (for example, 80% of Malaysians, 79% of Indonesians, 78% of Australians and 78% of Filipinos surveyed in 2013 said they viewed it positively).[65] However, the Chinese and South Koreans hold negative views of Japan (90% and 77% respectively), particularly owing to its perceived failure to atone sufficiently for past war crimes.[66] Visits by senior Japanese politicians (including Prime Minister Abe in December 2013) to memorials such as the Yasukuni shrine, which include tributes to war criminals, have only served to heighten these sentiments.

Japan's relationship with South Korea has experienced other difficulties too, owing to disputes over maritime claims and historical disputes over Second World War crimes. All these factors have thus far prevented any real collaboration between the two countries despite (in the minds of many outsiders) their having similar broad interests and concerns (with regard to North Korea and China in particular). In 2012, these disputes stymied a joint agreement on intelligence-sharing, and tensions have been increased since the election of nationalist leaders in Japan and South Korea in 2013.

Japan has emphasized better relations with India. Their first official trilateral dialogue with the United States was held in 2011 (although informal Track II meetings have been taking place since 2005).[67] The closeness was displayed when Prime Minister Abe was the chief guest at India's Republic Day celebrations in January 2014. Japan increasingly views India as a useful counterbalance to China's growing influence.

In a similar way, Japan views Australia as an effective and reliable partner for security cooperation and as a stable trade partner. In a reflection of the closeness of this relationship, Abe accepted an invitation from Prime Minister Abbott in 2013 for what would be the first state visit to Australia by a Japanese leader in 11 years and would include the first address by a Japanese prime minister before a joint sitting of the Australian parliament.[68]

Japan's relations with China have become increasingly strained and have focused on territorial disputes. While trade between the two remains strong, in recent years it has fallen (by 3.9% and 5.1% in 2012 and 2013 respectively).[69] However, it has been argued that 'an economic version of mutual deterrence' prevents the disputes from turning into active confrontation and, for the moment, the status quo seems to be holding firm.[70] But there are real risks of miscalculation and the potential for conflict between the two historical adversaries remains perhaps the biggest potential pitfall for regional stability.

> **Japan's relations with China have become increasingly strained and have focused on territorial disputes … the potential for conflict between the two historical adversaries remains perhaps the biggest potential pitfall for regional stability.**

Abe has made efforts to increase the strength of Japanese relations with other states in the region. For example, in July 2013 he made his third trip in the ASEAN region since resuming office.[71] That year marked the 40th anniversary of friendship and cooperation between Japan and ASEAN, and Japan signalled that it wished to deepen its relationship with its members (particularly in defence cooperation with Vietnam, Singapore, the Philippines and Indonesia).[72] Japan has also been keen for ASEAN countries to increase their defence spending and has assisted the Philippines in this effort by providing 10 naval vessels at no cost.[73]

US relations

Since the end of the Second World War, Japan and the United States have built a strong relationship, with treaties in 1954 and 1960 that obligate the latter to come to the former's aid if it comes under attack. Japan remains the key strategic base for the United States in the region:

---

[65] Pew Research, 'Japanese Public's Mood Rebounding, Abe Highly Popular', Survey Report, 11 July 2013, http://www.pewglobal.org/2013/07/11/japanese-publics-mood-rebounding-abe-strongly-popular/.

[66] Ibid.

[67] US Department of State, 'US-Japan-India Trilateral', Media Note, 19 December 2011, http://www.state.gov/r/pa/prs/ps/2011/12/179172.htm.

[68] Naomi Woodley, 'Prime Minister Tony Abbott holds first formal meeting with Japanese PM Shinzo Abe', ABC News, 10 October 2013, http://www.abc.net.au/news/2013-10-09/tony-abbott-png-trade-china-economy-brunei/5012868; 'Tony Abbott invites Shinzo Abe, saying Japan is Australia's "best friend in Asia"', The Guardian, 10 October 2013, http://www.theguardian.com/world/2013/oct/10/aboott-invites-abe-japan-friend.

[69] Gordon G. Chang, 'The Chinese And Japanese Economies Are Delinking: Prelude To Conflict?', Forbes, 16 February 2014, http://www.forbes.com/sites/gordonchang/2014/02/16/the-chinese-and-japanese-economies-are-delinking-prelude-to-conflict/.

[70] Richard Katz, 'Mutual Assured Production. Why Trade Will Limit Conflict Between China and Japan', Foreign Affairs, July/August 2013, http://www.foreignaffairs.com/articles/139451/richard-katz/mutual-assured-production.

[71] Daisuke Yamamoto, 'Solid ASEAN ties key to Abe strategy', Japan Times, 31 July 2013, http://www.japantimes.co.jp/news/2013/07/31/national/solid-asean-ties-key-to-abe-strategy/#.Uw4D7c4SrAo.

[72] Japanese Ministry of Defense, 'Defense of Japan 2013, Chapter 2 Initiatives to Further Stabilize the International Security Environment', pp. 239–41. http://www.mod.go.jp/e/publ/w_paper/pdf/2013/38_Part3_Chapter2_Sec2.pdf.

[73] Jane Perlez, 'China increases aid to Philippines', New York Times, 14 November 2013, http://www.nytimes.com/2013/11/15/world/asia/chinese-aid-to-philippines.html?hp&_r=0.

36,700 US personnel are stationed there, mainly on the island of Okinawa.[74] In 2013, Secretary of Defense Hagel increased troop levels there and agreed to strengthen the defence relationship with Japan through cooperation on new threats (such as in cyber security), to deploy advanced aircraft to Japan (such as MV-22 Ospreys), and to station a new ballistic missile defence radar in Kyogamisak.[75] In a statement on plans to relocate the US Marines' Futenma air base to Okinawa, Hagel stressed that America is committed to building 'a strong and sustainable US military presence' in Japan.[76] The two countries regularly conduct joint military exercises, and in what was widely viewed as a vote of confidence in Japan, its forces led part of the 2012 Rim of the Pacific (RIMPAC) exercises.[77]

Japan has been a key supporter of the United States' pivot to the region and broadly looks to it to resolve regional security issues and maintain stability. However, the pivot has not been without controversy. Recent comments by Secretary of State John Kerry aimed at reassuring Japan have only served to reinforce doubts. Speaking after meeting with his Japanese counterpart last year, he said:

> The United States, as everybody knows, does not take a position on the ultimate sovereignty of the [Senkaku/Diaoyu] islands. But we do recognize that they are under the administration of Japan. And we obviously want all the parties to deal with territorial issues through peaceful means [...] And so we oppose any unilateral or coercive action that would somehow aim at changing the status quo.[78]

While the United States had intended to be supportive, in practice many Japanese felt undermined by the ambiguity of Kerry's statement.[79]

The relationship is not without tensions, particularly with regard to the US bases and personnel – the environmental impact of the heavy air contingent has raised public protests, and perhaps more troubling have been the sex crimes committed by US personnel.[80] While the relationship is likely to remain strong, Japan does appear to have begun to diversify its security relationships with other states such as India, Australia and the Philippines.[81] This in part reflects growing Japanese anxiety over the relationship and perceptions of the changing global balance of power. On the other hand, at a high-level meeting between the two governments in October 2013, Japan agreed to deepen security cooperation with the United States in areas such as space, cyberspace, intelligence and surveillance.[82]

Singapore

Military budget 2013: $9.86bn

Military budget as a percentage of GDP: 3.4%

Active forces: 72,500 (Army 50,000; Navy 9,000; Air Force 13,500; Paramilitary 75,100; Reserve Forces: 312,500)

Despite Singapore's small size and population, it is seen as both a leading economy and perhaps the most strategically astute country in the region. Over the last five decades, it has developed from a small city to a state that punches far above its weight. It has developed a strong economy by becoming a regional trade and investment hub. However, its size makes it vulnerable, and it is reliant on others for a secure supply of basic goods such as water and other natural resources. As a result, Singapore faces a very different strategic environment from other countries in this study.

Regional relationships

Much like Indonesia, Singapore has an individual approach to managing the balance in its relations with the United States and China. It has played a very effective game, ensuring in its diplomacy that the two big powers do not see its situation as zero-sum. China views Singapore as an important trading partner, a hub for incoming oil and a useful model for economic development. China and Singapore also retain strong cultural ties, with Singapore's founder and former prime minister, Lee Kuan Yew, serving as mentor to many Chinese leaders. For example, China's

[74] IISS, *The Military Balance 2014*, p. 254.

[75] Karen Parrish, 'US, Japan Agree to Expand Security, Defense Cooperation', American Forces Press Service, 3 October 2013, http://www.defense.gov/news/newsarticle.aspx?id=120902.

[76] Kiyoshi Takenaka, 'Japan gets Okinawa approval for US Marine base move', Reuters, 27 December 2013, http://www.reuters.com/article/2013/12/27/us-japan-usa-okinawa-idUSBRE9BQ0AC20131227.

[77] Kirk Spitzer, 'Japan takes command – but don't tell anyone', *Time*, 28 June 2012, http://nation.time.com/2012/06/28/japan-takes-command-but-dont-tell-anyone/.

[78] US Department of State, 'Joint Press Availability With Japanese Foreign Minister Kishida After Their Meeting', 14 April 2013, http://www.state.gov/secretary/remarks/2013/04/207483.htm.

[79] Jacob M. Schlesinger and Alexander Martin, 'Kerry reassures Tokyo – but don't tell anyone', *Wall Street Journal*, 15 April 2013, http://blogs.wsj.com/japanrealtime/2013/04/15/kerry-reassures-tokyo-for-now/.

[80] Martin Fackler, 'Curfew is imposed on US military in Japan amid rape inquiries', *New York Times*, 19 October 2012, http://www.nytimes.com/2012/10/20/world/asia/curfew-imposed-on-american-troops-in-japan.html?_r=0.

[81] Swenson-Wright, *Is Japan Truly 'Back'?*

[82] Karen Parrish, 'US, Japan Agree to Expand Security, Defense Cooperation', American Forces Press Service, 3 October 2013, http://www.defense.gov/news/newsarticle.aspx?id=120902.

President, Xi Jinping, has referred to Lee as 'our senior who has our respect'.[83] However, relations between the two countries are not without strains and Singapore's long-standing military-to-military relationship with Taiwan has proved at times to be problematic.

Singapore has also developed good military-to-military relations with Thailand and India, which have allowed it to carry out exercises on their territory. It sees the strategic potential of India and has sought to emphasize more engagement. With regard to South Korea, Prime Minister Lee Hsien Loong stated in a recent bilateral meeting with President Park that he would like to see increased collaboration on areas such as construction, infrastructure, research and development, and doing business in third countries.[84]

In December 2009, Singapore signed a memorandum on defence cooperation with Japan – the first Southeast Asian country to do so. Both have promised to cooperate more closely on logistical support and joint exercises through the ADMM+ framework (see below).[85] Singapore and Australia have had a free trade agreement in operation since 2003 and have a strong economic relationship.[86] Military cooperation is also extensive, principally through the Five Powers Defence Agreement. Singapore has also provided support to Australian operations in Afghanistan.[87]

Singapore is the leading economy in ASEAN and sees a strong group as positive. It supports a more leading role for Indonesia in the organization. Singapore has also played a leading role in anti-piracy efforts both in the region and more broadly (for example, it has led three multinational operations in the Gulf of Aden).[88]

US relationship

As part of its strategy to manage relations with China and the United States, Singapore has never agreed to formal basing of the US military within its territory. However, by allowing the United States to use its naval and air facilities,

and with the recent addition of two littoral ships being stationed in Singapore in 2011, there is a *de facto* US base there. Singapore has not ruled out hosting Chinese ships if the request were to be made.

Singapore has a formal strategic partnership with the United States and remains one of the closest US allies within ASEAN.[89] As a small island state highly reliant on international trade, Singapore supports the US role in maintaining regional stability and keeping the sea lanes open.

South Korea

Military budget 2013: $31.8bn

Military budget as a percentage of GDP: 2.5%

Active forces: 655,000 (Army 522,000; Navy 68,000; Air Force 65,000; Paramilitary 4,500; Reserves 4,500,000)

Over the past four decades, South Korea has risen to become an economic power, technological innovator and strategic actor in the region. President Park Geun-hye, who took office in February 2013 and is the daughter of former president Park Chung-hee, has been beset by significant North Korean provocations, ranging from the ending of long-standing non-aggression pacts to threatening rhetoric.[90]

Regional relationships

China is a vital actor for South Korea's economic stability and security. Like many other countries, the latter is stuck between needing the United States for security purposes and being dependent on China economically. However, it is also reliant on China for its influence in North Korea. President Park's four-day trip to China in June 2013 underscored the importance of a trading relationship worth $256 billion a year.[91] In the same month, South Korea and

[83] Robert D. Blackwill and Graham Allison, 'Seek the wisdom of Lee Kuan Yew', Politico, 23 February 2013, http://www.politico.com/story/2013/02/seek-the-wisdomof-lee-kuan-yew-87620.html.
[84] Wi Tack-whan and Limb Jae-un, 'President Park holds summit with Singapore, Australia, Myanmar', Korea.net, 10 October 2013, http://www.korea.net/NewsFocus/Policies/view?articleId=113423.
[85] Japanese Ministry of Defense, 'Defense of Japan 2013, Chapter 2 Initiatives to Further Stabilize the International Security Environment', http://www.mod.go.jp/e/publ/w_paper/pdf/2013/38_Part3_Chapter2_Sec2.pdf, p. 240.
[86] The Australian Government, Australian Trade Commission, 'Singapore-Australia Free Trade Agreement SAFTA', http://www.austrade.gov.au/Export/About-Exporting/Trade-Agreements/SAFTA.
[87] The Australian Government, Minister for Foreign Affairs and Trade, 'Singapore Australia Joint Ministerial Committee', Media release, 26 July 2009, http://www.foreignminister.gov.au/releases/2009/fa-s090726.html.
[88] Walter Sim, 'SAF takes over command of multinational anti-piracy task force', *The Straits Times*, 7 March 2013, http://www.straitstimes.com/breaking-news/singapore/story/saf-takes-over-command-multinational-anti-piracy-task-force-20130307.
[89] Emma Chanlett-Avery, 'Singapore: Background and US Relations', Congressional Research Service, 26 July 2013, http://www.fas.org/sgp/crs/row/RS20490.pdf.
[90] 'How potent are North Korea's threats?', BBC News, 2 April 2013, http://www.bbc.co.uk/news/world-asia-21710644.
[91] Wang Haiqing, 'Commentary: Park's visit opens new chapter in China-South Korea relations', Xinhuanet, 27 June 2013, http://news.xinhuanet.com/english/indepth/2013-06/27/c_132490458.htm.

China also held their sixth high-level strategic dialogue in Beijing.[92] Interestingly, the two countries chose to make a very rare joint declaration condemning North Korea's nuclear activities during President Park's visit.[93] It has also been announced that they will launch a 2+2 consultative body to increase bilateral cooperation in the face of growing nuclear threats from North Korea.[94]

As mentioned above, despite their similar interests, South Korea's relationship with Japan is not as straightforward as many (particularly in the United States) would wish. Like others in Asia, South Koreans have negative memories and feelings towards Japan that can be traced back to the legacy of colonial subjugation and the crimes of the Second World War, and which are kept alive by the perceived lack of contrition on the Japanese side over issues including compensation for surviving South Korean 'comfort women'. Tensions have been raised more recently by Prime Minister Abe's stated intention to increase Japanese military capabilities and South Korea's new concern that Japan is rising again militarily.

South Korea and Australia are working towards completing a free-trade agreement and have emphasized the importance of reaching a peaceful solution for the Korean peninsula.[95] In July 2013, their foreign and defence ministers held the first 2+2 meeting and pledged to work together and to improve bilateral defence cooperation in areas such as joint exercises, people-to-people links, joint operations on maritime security, peacekeeping operations, humanitarian assistance and disaster relief, and better cooperation on cyberspace and space security.[96]

Relations between ASEAN and South Korea have expanded in recent years diplomatically and in terms of trade. South Korea has also cooperated with Indonesia in developing the latter's maritime and aerial capabilities.[97] And there were calls in 2013 to deepen the relationship to deal with emerging challenges such as cyber crime and peace-keeping.[98]

US relationship

Since the end of the Korean War in 1953, the United States has been the principal guarantor of South Korea's security. Treaties and agreements signed in 1950 and 1953 form the foundation of their bilateral alliance. The United States currently stations 28,500 troops in the country, many along the heavily fortified border with North Korea, and an additional 800 were announced in January 2014.[99] It also maintains wartime command of South Korean forces through the Combined Forces Command structure, although this is supposed to be transferred to Seoul in 2015 (a move that was delayed from 2012). In July 2013 South Korea requested a further delay in the handover of command beyond December 2015.[100] This reflected growing anxiety over North Korean provocation and continued dependence on the US alliance. The North Korean crisis of 2013 and the ongoing uncertainty surrounding the likely actions of the new North Korean leader, Kim Jong-Un, have served to reinforce the security relationship with the United States, although many South Koreans express some uncertainty over continued US reliability.

Major regional organizations

The Asia-Pacific region is host to a complex series of regional organizations with often vaguely delineated and overlapping substantive remits and memberships. For over 50 years these have been used as forums for regional discussion, assisted in disaster relief and facilitated diplomatic engagement.

ASEAN, the most active of these organizations, was founded in 1967 to deal with the threat of communism and promote economic development. It has since spawned a number of related groupings such as ASEAN+1 (multiple versions), ASEAN+3 (with China, Japan and South Korea), the ASEAN Defence Ministers Meeting (ADMM) and the ADMM+

[92] 'China, ROK hold high-level strategic dialogue', Xinhuanet, 4 June 2013, http://news.xinhuanet.com/english/china/2013-06/04/c_124811700.htm.
[93] Choe Sang-Hun, 'China and South Korea reaffirm efforts aimed at North', New York Times, 27 June 2013, http://www.nytimes.com/2013/06/28/world/asia/china-and-south-korea-reaffirm-efforts-to-end-north-koreas-nuclear-threat.html?_r=1&.
[94] 'S. Korea, China to launch "two-plus-two" security talks by year-end', Yonhap News Agency, 21 October 2013, http://english.yonhapnews.co.kr/national/2013/10/21/84/0301000000AEN20131021006800315F.html.
[95] Wi Tack-whan, Limb Jae-un, 'President Park holds summit with Singapore, Australia, Myanmar', Korea.net, 10 October 2013, http://www.korea.net/NewsFocus/Policies/view?articleId=113423.
[96] The Australian Government, 'Minister for Foreign Affairs and Minister for Defence – Joint Statement – Australia-Republic of Korea Foreign and Defence Ministers' 2+2 Meeting', 4 July 2013, http://www.minister.defence.gov.au/2013/07/04/minister-for-foreign-affairs-and-minister-for-defence-joint-statement-australia-republic-of-korea-foreign-and-defence-ministers-22-meeting/.
[97] Arnaud Leveau, 'Relationships between South Korea and ASEAN countries,' Academia.edu, 29 March 2011, http://www.academia.edu/1688487/Relationships_between_South_Korea_and_ASEAN_countries.
[98] Novan Iman Santosa and Yuliasri Perdani, 'S. Korea, Indonesia urged to deepen defense cooperation', Jakarta Post, 3 May 2013, http://www.thejakartapost.com/news/2013/05/03/s-korea-indonesia-urged-deepen-defense-cooperation.html.
[99] IISS, The Military Balance 2014, p. 260; and 'United States sending more troops and tanks to South Korea', Reuters, 7 January 2014, http://www.reuters.com/article/2014/01/08/us-korea-usa-troops-idUSBREA061AU20140108.
[100] Jeyup S. Kwaak, 'Seoul asks US to delay transfer of military command', Wall Street Journal, 17 July 2013, http://online.wsj.com/news/articles/SB10001424127887324448104578611172058809496?mg=reno64-wsj&url=http%3A%2F%2Fonline.wsj.com%2Farticle%2FSB10001424127887324448104578611172058809496.html.

(which includes defence ministers from additional countries, including the United States). There is also the ASEAN Regional Forum (ARF), which focuses on security issues.

Outside ASEAN and related sub-entities there are other regional forums such as Asia-Pacific Economic Cooperation (APEC), the East Asia Summit (EAS), the South Asian Association for Regional Cooperation (SAARC), the Bay of Bengal Initiative for Multi-Sectoral Technical and Economic Cooperation (BIMSTEC) and the Shanghai Cooperation Organization (SCO). Some of these have different centres of gravity, such as India for BIMSTEC and China and Russia for the SCO, and can have a specific thematic focus (e.g. the ADMM on defence cooperation and APEC on economic development). (See Appendix for further details on the membership and aspirations of each of the regional groups.)

Over recent decades these groups have grown not just in size but also in terms of the complexity and variety of challenges they seek to tackle. While ASEAN was developed in the Cold War era of economic division and during China's Cultural Revolution, these groups today face a rising China and growing regional tensions, along with more regional interdependence and economic development.

The Asia-Pacific region probably accounts for the highest number and variety of major regional organizations in the world. They are often criticized for overlapping and, in some cases, being superfluous. They also have a reputation for being talking shops with little practical operational function.[101] Critics point to a perceived lack of concrete accomplishments and to institutions riven with internal divisions that prevent decisive action. As ASEAN and the other major regional organizations are consensus-driven, the objections of only one member can create paralysis on an issue (such as Cambodia's effective veto on the 2012 final joint ASEAN statement). Moreover, in comparison with their Western counterparts, particularly NATO and the EU, it is hard to view them as operational entities.

On the other hand, it may be too much to expect European levels of cooperation in an area as economically, ethnically, politically and geographically diverse as this. It should also be recognized that significant advances have been made since the founding of ASEAN. These groups provide a valuable stepping stone to further advances in cooperation and collaboration as the Asia-Pacific countries find areas of mutual interest in which to work together.

Figure 2: Overlapping organizations in the Asia-Pacific region

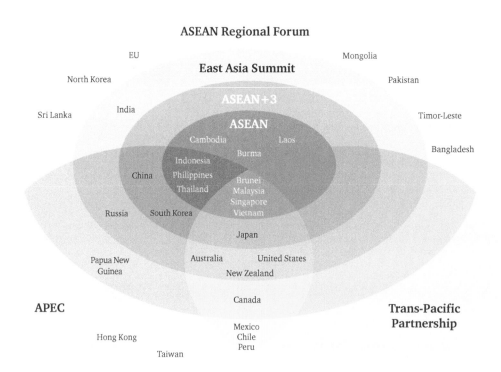

Source: Authors.

[101] 'Asean Front and Center', *Asia Sentinel*, 7 September 2012, http://www.asiasentinel.com/politics/asean-front-and-center/.

3. Threats

When viewed from a broad high-level perspective, there is great commonality of security interests and concerns among the states studied in this report. They pay significant attention to the balance between the two largest actors in the region – China and the United States – and the repercussions of their actions on issues ranging from trade to maintaining open sea lanes and ensuring safe and secure (and clearly delineated) borders. North Korea's nuclear weapons capabilities also figure prominently in the thinking of a number of these countries. At a more granular level, however, major differences emerge between their respective analyses of threats.

Consideration of security interests and threats can be explored from two perspectives: the actor or scenario causing the threat or concern, and the mechanism or lever by which pressure or influence is exerted.

The actors and scenarios

All six countries in this report see the emergence of China as a major power in the region (and beyond) as a principal concern or interest to be managed. At the same time and to varying degrees, however, China is also one of their foremost trading partners and, in some cases, an important investor.[102] As a result, each country has a somewhat different balance with regard to whether it sees China more as an opportunity or as a challenge. This leads each to follow a separate path in terms of its bilateral engagement with China, as well as with the United States and other regional powers. These divergent views have significant and broad implications for their ability to work together with respect to China and for the efficacy of regional organizations.

The place of China in the security analyses of the six countries encompasses many aspects, from managing the bilateral US–Chinese relationship to dealing with China as an emerging power, to its role in engaging with North Korea (above and beyond China's participation in the Six-Party Talks). The following five actors or scenarios encompass the major concerns raised by the six states investigated.

Managing the US–Chinese relationship

For most of the six countries, the foremost security concern is not a rising China, but how to maintain the balance between it and the United States. China is a vital economic partner, for many of them the largest, while the United States provides security to the region and in some cases is a formal alliance partner. It is thus crucial to all Asia-Pacific countries that they maintain positive and productive relations with both powers.

To this end they are extremely sensitive to changes in the US–Chinese relationship. On the one hand, it is important that this relationship remains positive: they want, more than anything, not to have to choose between the two countries. On the other hand, they do not want the relationship to be too close as they fear then that they may play second fiddle to China's interests in the minds of American policy-makers. (The possibility of a G2, which was briefly debated in 2009, raised many hackles in the region.) This leaves them hoping for a 'Goldilocks-like' middle ground in which the relationship is neither too hot nor too cold.

Table 1: Prioritization of security threats by country

	An assertive China (militarily and/or economically)	Closing of sea lanes/trade	North Korea (collapse, nuclear assertiveness or proliferation)	Terrorism/ insurgency	Resource scarcity	Border security/ territorial integrity
Australia	***	**			*	***
India	***	*		***	*	**
Indonesia	*	*		***	**	**
Japan	***	***	**		*	***
Singapore	*	*			*	
South Korea	**	**	***			**

Key

* Low priority
** Medium priority
*** High priority

102 Central Intelligence Agency, *World Factbook*, 'Imports', https://www.cia.gov/library/publications/the-world-factbook/fields/2061.html, and *World Factbook*, 'Exports', https://www.cia.gov/library/publications/the-world-factbook/fields/2050.html. 'China's overseas investment, ODI-lay hee-ho', *The Economist*, 19 January 2013, http://www.economist.com/news/china/21569775-expanding-scale-and-scope-chinas-outward-direct-investment-odi-lay-hee-ho; and for Singapore, see Rajeshni Naidu-Ghelani, 'Top 10 Countries for Chinese Investments', CNBC, 24 May 2012, http://www.cnbc.com/id/47512207/page/6.

In addition to the complexities this balance requires, the focus on the US–Chinese relationship could also potentially create a Cold War-like situation where relations are zero-sum. This could raise tensions between the two countries that serve no one's interests. Yet, despite this, for many countries in the region this is exactly the dilemma into which they are driving the two major powers.

> The focus on the US–Chinese relationship could also potentially create a Cold War-like situation where relations are zero-sum. This could raise tensions between the two countries that serve no one's interests.

Meanwhile, the US 'pivot' to the region has elevated concerns rather than alleviated them. The intention was to reassure allies that the United States intended to remain strongly engaged in Asia and to ensure that the smaller regional powers were not pressured by others into taking steps or giving up territory against their will. However, given perceived mixed messages from senior US officials over the past two years, this has not been the result. Instead, the rebalancing has in many cases heightened concerns in the region, particularly with the initial focus on the military aspect, raising fears that China would become antagonized and respond to what it might perceive as containment. (In the eyes of many, this has indeed been the Chinese response.) The United States appears to have had very mixed success in its efforts to reassure friends and partners in the region about its continued staying power and commitment.[103]

The US–Chinese relationship has been at the top of the regional security agenda and one of the principal strategic challenges for all but Singapore and Indonesia. Singapore, perhaps because of its small geographic size (making it no threat) and its strong economic base, expresses great confidence in its ability to withstand any pressures imposed by these two main powers.[104] Its leaders exude faith in their ability to balance between the two and they eschew the bipolar narrative. Their skill at doing so is demonstrated by their ability to preserve major US naval capabilities in the country (though explicitly not US bases) without inducing a Chinese response. China apparently understands the intentional ambiguity here and accepts it. Thus Singapore avoids the need to provide similar treatment to both countries and skirts the issue of balance.

Indonesia avoids this dilemma through a different strategy. Its role as co-founder of the NAM permits it to avoid commitment to either China or the United States. Strategically, it uses ASEAN to focus and engage on issues beyond its borders and only acts unilaterally on internal security concerns such as regarding the risk of insurgency. By working in this way in a consensus-driven organization, Indonesia too can avoid the need for balance and being susceptible to pressure from either the United States or China.

A rising China

In the minds of many, China is the leader of the emerging BRICS countries.[105] Recent polls have suggested that in many countries China is perceived as already surpassing the United States in power and influence.[106] In Asia, however, opinions are more mixed. Majorities in China, South Korea and Australia believe that China has replaced or will one day replace the United States as the world's leading power (66%, 56% and 67% respectively).[107] In Japan, Malaysia, the Philippines and Indonesia, however, this opinion is held by far smaller percentages of the population (24%, 30%, 22% and 39% respectively). Trends indicate that the perception that the United States is being replaced by China has increased steadily since the 2008 financial crisis hit the West, leaving China and the other emerging nations as the principal drivers of economic growth.[108] Despite the relatively recent slowdown in China's economic growth, this perception continues.

China's military growth and assertiveness

China's military growth is being watched very closely in the region and beyond. According to official figures, its annual defence spending has grown by double-digit percentages almost every year since 1989. Most estimates take the figure to be higher. While over half of this is spent on internal security, it is still notably more than any of its neighbours.[109]

---

[103] This lack of reassurance came across in multiple interviews and discussions in the region from representatives from government as well as outside it, the media, academia and elsewhere.

[104] Although there are suggestions by some that that this confidence could be quite superficial.

[105] This terminology was created in 2001 by Goldman Sachs to refer to the major rising powers – Brazil, Russia, India and China. South Africa was subsequently added to the list.

[106] 'America's Global Image Remains More Positive than China's', Pew Research Global Attitudes Project, 18 July 2013, http://www.pewglobal.org/2013/07/18/chapter-4-global-balance-of-power/#u-s-and-chinese-influence-in-asia.

[107] Ibid.

[108] Pew Research surveyed 20 countries in 2008 and 2013, and found that the median percentage asserting China as the 'world's leading economic power' increased from 20% to 34%. At the same time, the figure for the United States has fallen from 47% to 41%. Andrew Hammond, 'China Is Increasingly Seen as the #1 Power, and That's a Problem for China', Forbes, 9 May 2013, http://www.forbes.com/sites/realspin/2013/09/05/china-is-increasingly-seen-as-the-1-power-and-thats-a-problem-for-china/.

[109] Calum MacLeod, 'China boosts military and domestic security spending', USA Today, 5 March 2013, http://www.usatoday.com/story/news/world/2013/03/05/china-party-congress-military/1964405/.

It is estimated that in 2013 China's military expenditure was $112 billion while the next largest spenders in Asia were Japan ($51 billion) and India ($36 billion).[110] However, estimates vary considerably, and according to the Stockholm Institute for International Peace Research, the Chinese figure may be significantly higher (see Figure 3). Meanwhile, China is also building new capabilities to operate out of area, with the launch of its first aircraft carrier in 2011, and it is also working to deny others access to its immediate neighbourhood through anti-access/area denial (A2/AD) capabilities.[111] It is also increasingly focused on developing its cyber capabilities.[112]

Figure 3: Asia-Pacific defence spending (selected countries)

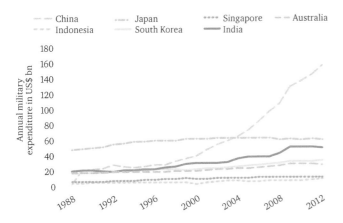

Source: SIPRI Military Expenditure Database, http://www.sipri.org/research/armaments/milex/milex_database/milex_database.

At the same time, it should be noted that, despite its rapid growth, no estimates see China overtaking US defence spending until 2025, and it will take far longer (if ever) for it to develop traditional capabilities (such as in the naval arena) to match those of the United States.[113] For example, China has one active aircraft carrier to America's 11 (it is currently building another and the United States is considering refurbishing one). China does not have access (and is unlikely to do so in the near term) to a

global network of bases and allies comparable to the size of America's. It also lacks the vast combat and operational experience of the US military.

As China's capabilities increase, so does its will to use them. Traditionally a land power, China is trying to expand its zone of control in the maritime and air arenas in ways not seen before. Since early 2010, it has taken a more assertive military posture, sending its navy to confront other countries' fishing, surveying or other vessels, including in particular those from Japan and the Philippines, in the South and East China Seas.[114] In September 2010, the Japanese Coast Guard arrested the captain of a Chinese fishing vessel that had rammed two of its ships; the Chinese response included threats to suspend high-level negotiations and the cessation of shipments of rare-earth minerals to Japan.[115]

In 2012, China again showed its willingness to assert itself militarily. In April, it took a strong position against the Philippines regarding the latter's interception of eight Chinese fishing vessels around the disputed Scarborough Shoal, to which the Chinese military continues to prevent access. In September 2012, when the Japanese government nationalized the Senkaku/Diaoyu Islands, China responded by raising the level of patrols to the area far beyond those seen historically, and making a strong diplomatic protest (there were also major demonstrations in China against Japan and Japanese companies).[116]

In late 2013, tensions again escalated when China unilaterally imposed an air defence identification zone (ADIZ) incorporating territory disputed by both Japan and South Korea, noting that aircraft travelling through the zone without permission would be subject to the use of 'emergency defensive measures' by the Chinese military.[117] South Korea subsequently took a similar step, raising even further the potential for a dangerous miscalculation. The United States, Japan and South Korea have sent aircraft through the ADIZ since, without incurring a response from China. In December 2013, US and Chinese ships almost collided when a US ship monitoring a Chinese carrier had to take evasive action to avoid a Chinese patrol.[118] In February 2014, the Chinese

[110] Malaysia spent $5bn, Australia $26 bn, South Korea $31,8bn and Singapore $9,86bn. IISS, *The Military Balance 2014*, pp. 261, 223, 257, 275.

[111] Chris Buckley, 'China launches first aircraft carrier on maiden sea trial', Reuters, 10 August 2011, http://www.reuters.com/article/2011/08/10/us-china-military-carrier-idUSTRE77900D20110810.

[112] 'China boosts defense spending as military modernizes arsenal', Bloomberg News, 5 March 2013, http://www.bloomberg.com/news/2013-03-05/china-boosts-defense-spending-as-military-modernizes-its-arsenal.html.

[113] Giri Rajendran, 'Chinese-US defence spending projections', IISS Voices, 19 March 2013, http://iissvoicesblog.wordpress.com/2013/03/19/chinese-us-defence-spending-projections/.

[114] Robert Maginnis 'China's High Seas Aggression', Human Events, 20 May 2010, http://www.humanevents.com/2010/05/20/chinas-high-seas-aggression/.

[115] Raul Pedrozo, 'Beijing's Coastal Real Estate', *Foreign Affairs*, 15 November 2010, http://www.foreignaffairs.com/articles/67007/raul-pedrozo/beijings-coastal-real-estate.

[116] 'China warns of consequences as Japan announces purchase of disputed islands', *The Guardian*, 11 September 2012, http://www.theguardian.com/world/2012/sep/11/china-warns-japan-disputed-islands and 'The Senkaku/Diaoyu islands, Dangerous shoals', *The Economist*, 17 January 2013, http://www.economist.com/news/leaders/21569740-risks-clash-between-china-and-japan-are-risingand-consequences-could-be.

[117] 'China outlines E China Sea air defense identification zone', Xinhuanet, 23 November 2011, http://news.xinhuanet.com/english/video/2013-11/23/c_132912297.htm.

[118] Sui-Lee Wee, 'China confirms near miss with US ship in South China Sea', Reuters, 18 December 2013, http://www.reuters.com/article/2013/12/18/us-china-usa-ships-idUSBRE9BH03M20131218.

military surprised Australia's government by conducting military exercises closer than ever before to Australian territory, between Indonesia and Christmas Island.[119]

These actions, and others, 'have raised concerns in many countries of the region not just over the increasing disparity between their military capabilities and those of China, but also over the latter's relatively new-found will to use such military strength to achieve its regional objectives. To many, the long-standing dictum of former president Hu Jintao about a 'peaceful Chinese development' is no longer an accurate representation of China's intent in the region. Its recent actions raise the chance of unintended conflict following a miscalculation on one side or the other.

Concerns about China's enhanced military capabilities have varied from country to country across the region. Inevitably, they are highest among those with which it is involved in major territorial disputes – India, Japan, the Philippines, Vietnam, Brunei, Malaysia and Taiwan – but much lower in Singapore and Indonesia. One study showed that Japanese and Indian elites tended to see China as both the greatest threat to peace but also as potentially the biggest force for peace.[120]

China's growing economic power

At the same time as it is expanding its military capabilities, China has also become a vital global economic power. As already noted, its GDP has grown annually by an average of over 10% (although in 2013 growth was only 7.7%) over the last decade, overtaking Japan to become the second largest economy in the world.[121] It is on track to surpass the United States in purchasing power parity (PPP) by 2018. China is now the largest merchandise exporter, second-largest merchandise importer, second-largest destination of foreign direct investment (FDI), largest manufacturer, largest holder of foreign exchange reserves, and largest creditor nation in the world.[122]

While this strong growth has been a benefit to many Asia-Pacific countries by lifting the region's overall economic growth, it also makes them increasingly dependent on China. As the largest exporting trade partner for five of the six countries considered here (Singapore being the exception), China's strong economic negotiating position makes them vulnerable to pressure.[123] Japan, South Korea and Australia (where China, its biggest two-way trading partner, accounts for 20% of its trade) are particularly sensitive to such pressure.[124]

Not only has China's importance as a trading partner grown following the 2008 Western economic downturn, it has also increasingly used its economic influence and leverage to achieve broader geopolitical as well as security interests (as shown, for example, in its decision to cut off exports of rare-earth minerals to Japan after the latter seized a Chinese fishing boat captain in September 2010).

China is also increasingly an important investor in many of these countries. In the case of Australia, while Chinese investment still accounts for only approximately 3% of total FDI, this is disproportionally focused in the west of the country, making many in that region feel uncomfortably vulnerable to any potential Chinese coercion.[125] In response, the province's leaders are exploring how to diversify and, where possible, expand their investor base to provide some cushioning against any future Chinese action.

China's regional leverage

In large part because of its growing military and its formidable economic power, China is increasingly using broader geopolitical leverage to achieve its regional objectives. In July 2012, for the first time in ASEAN's history, foreign ministers were unable to agree on a meeting's closing statement (given differences over the South China Sea conflicts that China does not want to be addressed in a multilateral forum) Cambodia refused to sign off on the consensus document, on direction (explicit or implicit) from its close associate, China. This was widely condemned internationally (to such an extent that some in China felt that perhaps it had gone too far). However, China effectively used its geopolitical leverage to block regional consensus on the final statement.

[119] David Wroe, 'RAAF scrambles plane to observe Chinese naval exercise', *Sydney Morning Herald*, 13 February 2014, http://www.smh.com.au/federal-politics/political-news/raaf-scrambles-plane-to-observe-chinese-naval-exercise-20140212-32ief.html.
[120] Centre for Strategic and International Studies, 'Strategic Views on Asian Regionalism', February 2009, p. 7, http://csis.org/files/media/csis/pubs/090217_gill_stratviews_web.pdf.
[121] World Bank, GDP current US$ as of February 2014, http://data.worldbank.org/indicator/NY.GDP.MKTP.CD; 'China trade rebounds in further sign economy stabilizing', Bloomberg News, 9 September 2013, http://www.bloomberg.com/news/2013-09-08/china-trade-rebounds-in-further-sign-economy-stabilizing.html.
[122] Wayne M. Morrison, 'China's Economic Rise: History, Trends, Challenges, and Implications for the United States', Congressional Research Service, 3 July 2013, http://fpc.state.gov/documents/organization/212020.pdf.
[123] CIA, *World Factbook*, 'Imports – Partners', as of February 2014, https://www.cia.gov/library/publications/the-world-factbook/fields/2061.html; and *World Factbook*, 'Exports –Partners', as of February 2014, https://www.cia.gov/library/publications/the-world-factbook/fields/2050.html.
[124] Australian Government Department of Foreign Affairs and Trade, 'Trade at a Glance 2013', as of February 2014, p. 16, http://www.dfat.gov.au/publications/trade/trade-at-a-glance-2013/.
[125] Australian Trade Commission, 'Foreign investment in Australia up 8.6pc in 2012', May 2013, http://www.austrade.gov.au/ArticleDocuments/3814/Data-Alert-130522-FDI-Increases.pdf.aspx.

China has also continued to play a strong role in supporting North Korea and in facilitating the Six-Party Talks with Western and Asian powers.[126] However, since the succession of Kim Jong-Un as leader in late 2010, there is mounting concern in China, as well as internationally, that its former influence is diminishing. Kim has ignored China's wishes on a number of occasions (not least when North Korea conducted a third nuclear test in February 2013), and concerns were particularly conspicuous in December 2013 following the arrest and subsequent execution of Kim's uncle (and previous mentor), with whom China had strong relations.[127] Perhaps as a result, more recently China has supported the broader international consensus on North Korea. However, it appears loath to test out its perhaps diminishing authority and influence in the country.

China's influence over North Korea and its leadership is particularly important to South Korea, which remains concerned about the possibility of a North Korean attack across the 38th Parallel, as well as by the consequences of a collapse of the regime including the possible reunification of the two Koreas. South Korea sees China as holding the key to preventing or managing both these potential events (particularly the latter), and this, more than anything, drives its strong desire to maintain a robust and positive relationship with Beijing. If, however, China's influence in North Korea continues to diminish, this could change.

Danger of Chinese collapse

Viewed as a low risk, but with a huge potential impact, is the possibility that China might falter rather than continue to rise, and perhaps even implode. Despite its impressive growth, there is a danger in 'straight-line thinking', a concern emphasized by China's recent slowing growth. Anxiety over the slow-down is found not just among China's leaders, who have publicly lamented that growth remains 'unbalanced, uncoordinated and unsustainable', but throughout the region, which would inevitably be affected by consequent decreases in trade and investment.[128]

China faces a host of domestic challenges – many of which its leadership has publicly acknowledged – including an ageing population, increasing demands from the middle class, growing political dissent, a property bubble and corruption.[129] While there are few signs that any downturn or collapse is imminent, given the challenges and the lack

of an escape valve for tensions within the country (such as meaningful elections), concerns are increasingly voiced that China has significant problems that could lead to instability. Unrest would inevitably have a large effect beyond the country's borders.

If an economic downturn or another equally significant event were to spiral out of control, a likely last-gasp solution for the Chinese leadership would be to divert its public's attention to an outside enemy, whether the United States, Japan or another. It is at such a juncture that long-standing tensions in the region would be most likely to escalate into a real conflict between China and another state. A collapse of the Chinese state, with all the uncertainty, unrest and possible migration and refugee flows that might result, would have global repercussions too as a new regional power balance developed and a country with over 1.3 billion people worked through massive disruptions and potential violence.

While this scenario is unlikely, it nevertheless remains in the back of the minds of many senior policy-makers and academics in the region.

Uncertainty over North Korea

North Korea's stability and the actions of its leadership and military are concerns raised in particular by the Northeast Asian states among those considered here, and are most acutely felt by South Korea. There are three elements to the perceived threat.

Cross-border attack

In March 2010, North Korea sank a South Korean navy ship by firing a torpedo from a mini-submarine. In November of the same year, it shelled the South Korean island of Yeonpyeong. South Korea responded by firing on North Korean gun positions.

South Korea took a number of additional steps in response to these two incidents. It asked the United States to retain military control of the Combined Forces Command at least until 2015 (and it has since requested another delay).[130] It also spelled out a new set of explicit 'immediate and strong counterattacks' to future provocations.[131] Thus any future attack of this kind by North Korea is likely to lead to a significantly stronger response.

---

126 Members of the Six-Party Talks are North Korea, South Korea, China, the United States, Japan and Russia.

127 David Sanger, 'North Korea confirms it conducted 3rd nuclear test', *New York Times*, 11 February 2013, www.nytimes.com/2013/02/12/world/asia/north-korea-nuclear-test.html.

128 Hu Jintao,' Report to 18th National Congress of the Communist Party of China', Xinhuanet, 8 November 2012, http://news.xinhuanet.com/english/special/18cpcnc/2012-11/17/c_131981259.htm.

129 Andrew Nathan and Andrew Scobell, *China's Search for Security* (Columbia University Press, 2012).

130 Craig Whitlock, 'South Korea wants US to keep control over combined wartime defence forces', *The Guardian*, 8 October 2013, http://www.theguardian.com/world/2013/oct/08/korea-south-north-us-military-chuck-hagel.

131 'S.Korea, US to keep combined forces command', *Chosun Ilbo*, 2 April 2013, http://english.chosun.com/site/data/html_dir/2013/04/02/2013040200626.html.

While the rising North Korean rhetoric in April and May 2013 (including a recommendation that foreign embassies evacuate so as not to be caught in any coming conflagration) was largely shrugged off by the diplomatic and financial community, any attack on South Korea would activate a new level of response. Given the ebb and flow in relations between the two countries, the possibility of another such attack is still uppermost in the minds of many South Koreans. Despite some small improvements in relations recently (such as the reopening of the Kaesong industrial park), they have little confidence that there is a permanent change in North Korean attitudes.[132]

While deemed unlikely, there is also some concern that an even more aggressive posture by Kim Jong-Un might lead to an attack across the 38th Parallel. This possibility is raised intermittently by North Korean leaders, such as in March 2013 when Pyongyang warned that the Korean peninsula was entering 'a state of war' and that 'provocations will not be limited to a local war, but develop into an all-out war, a nuclear war'.[133] Thus an attack by North Korea remains a possibility for which the South Korean military must plan.

Japan is the only other country, among those considered in this study, that prioritizes North Korean aggressiveness. This stems in part from the lack of closure on the cases of North Korea's abduction of Japanese citizens between 1977 and 1983. Its invasion of Japanese airspace during its missile tests also raises tension, as may Japan's close relationship with the United States, which some Japanese believe makes the country a target for North Korean aggression.

North Korean collapse

South Korea is also extremely sensitive to the possibility in the coming decade of a collapse of the North Korean regime. While there are few indications that this is imminent, North Korea's economic and resource challenges, combined with the growing realization among many of its citizens of the disparity in living standards between the north and south, increasingly raise the possibility that the population might eventually get desperate enough to take action against the regime. The other possibility, albeit now less likely following the humiliation and execution of Kim's uncle and the ongoing military shake-up, is a coup.

If the North Korean regime collapses, the impact on its two immediate neighbours, China and South Korea, will be huge. The influx of refugees, with its related humanitarian and economic crisis, will have long-term and significant implications for both and is one reason why China continues to support the North Korean regime. The presence of nuclear weapons will also ensure international engagement. How such a scenario would play out – whether North Korea remains an independent country or is reunified with South Korea – is in large part in the hands of China. South Korea's priority is thus to maintain positive relations with China and persuade it that reunification would not lead to the presence of an American satellite state on its border.

North Korean proliferation

Finally, North Korea has also threatened and acted to proliferate nuclear and missile technology.[134] This is one of its few sources of international revenue and thus, despite comprehensive sanctions, it continues to attempt such sales (e.g. to Syria and, most likely, Iran).[135] However, North Korea is increasingly being squeezed in this respect. As China takes a firmer stance towards the country's obstinacy and unwillingness to listen to advice, it is more willing to sign up to stronger international UN sanctions. At the same time, initiatives such as the Proliferation Security Initiative (PSI), launched in 2003, have proved quite effective, most recently in July 2013, when Panama seized a North Korean ship transporting missiles and other arms from Cuba for repairs in North Korea. Such efforts make it much harder for North Korea to continue selling its technology.

Terrorism and insurgency

The threat from terrorism, since its peak after the 2002 Bali bombings, appears to have diminished, in part owing to the capture or killing of many of terrorist leaders, but it remains of concern in the region. For example, the Philippines-based group Abu Sayyaf which once caused significant fears, has shrunk considerably since the early 2000s. The exception to this is in India, where the threat from Kashmiri militants remains ever-present.

Insurgency, on the other hand, continues to be of significant concern to several of the countries studied here. Indonesia, in particular, sees breakaway groups in the archipelago as

---

[132] Tom Phillips, 'South and North Korean strike a deal to reopen Kaesong industrial zone', *Daily Telegraph*, 7 July 2013, www.telegraph.co.uk/news/worldnews/asia/northkorea/10164919/South-and-North-Korean-strike-a-deal-to-reopen-Kaesong-industrial-zone.html.

[133] David Randall, 'North Korea crisis: Kim Jong-un threatens "all-out nuclear war"', *The Independent*, 31 March 2013, www.independent.co.uk/news/world/asia/north-korea-crisis-kim-jongun-threatens-allout-nuclear-war-8555350.html.

[134] North Korea also continues to use its own nuclear weapons production as a lever in negotiations in the Six-Party Talks. As recently as September 2013, reports surfaced that North Korea has restarted the Yongbyon nuclear reactor.

[135] David Albright, 'A Dangerous Nexus: Preventing Iran-Syria-North Korea Nuclear and Missile Proliferation', Institute for Science and International Security, 11 April 2013, http://isis-online.org/uploads/conferences/documents/Testimony_House_Subcommittees_11April2013_final.pdf.

presenting a major threat to its cohesiveness. The example of East Timor, which gained independence from Indonesia in 2002, continues to rankle and raises the spectre that others will try to pursue similar paths. Although Jakarta reached agreement on increased autonomy with the province of Aceh in 2005, tensions still pervade their relations. Groups within the province of Irian Jaya also continue to work towards greater independence or autonomy.

In India, Prime Minister Manmohan Singh has described insurgency, in the form of the Naxalites, as 'the greatest threat to our internal security'.[136] Despite the continued terrorist threat in Kashmir, the ongoing insurgency along India's eastern border results in a steady drip of killings and terrorist acts. Despite attempts by successive governments to resolve this insurgency, there appears to have been little change on the ground.

Points of leverage and pressure

Security threats, particularly between states, have historically played out in traditional ways, through air, sea and ground warfare or through defensive strategies. It is therefore unsurprising that the security capabilities of the six countries considered here have focused on a traditional range of assets, training and other resources. The swiftly rising military spending in Asia (China and India were the two highest defence spenders among developing countries in 2013) is indicative of the continued tension in this area.[137]

In an evaluation of each country's security resources, it is necessary to take into consideration not just troops numbers but also advances in their training and in the equipment they use, and thus in their inherent capabilities. For example, while the numbers of US troops in the region have largely held steady in recent decades, their capabilities have multiplied many-fold. Equally, while China now has a naval carrier, as it does not have the planes or the personnel with the training to operate effectively out of the carrier, this particular resource cannot be regarded as equal to that of a country with long-standing capacity in this area.

Security can no longer be thought of effectively within its more narrow traditional definition, however. It increasingly encompasses a more complex set of issues and a wider range of threats. The range of traditional and newer threats and levers in and for the Asia-Pacific region is considered below.

Resource insecurity

Environmental factors will play a key role in the ability of Asian countries to meet their future resource needs, whether with regard to food, water or other requirements. Climate-change impacts and environmental degradation trends are increasingly worrying, and will be exacerbated by rising resource use in many countries. These pressures will affect all countries in the region to varying degrees and are already presenting a greater number of cross-border challenges, whether it is Chinese coal-burning, Indonesian forest fires or perceptions of inequality over access to transboundary water.

Food

Over recent years the prices of basic foods globally have fluctuated significantly. In the 2007–08 price crisis the cost of certain foods tripled over a few months and left even Qatar (which has the richest population in the world) unable to secure its rice supply.[138] In 2010–11, Russia and Ukraine imposed export bans following a poor wheat harvest; the subsequent price spike has been identified by some as a contributing factor to the Arab uprisings.[139]

A large number of Asians are enjoying a much richer diet than has been the case historically. In 1982, an average Chinese person consumed only 13 kilos of meat per year; the Chinese now eat four times as much and consume a quarter of the world's meat supply.

As Asia's population and economic development has grown rapidly over the last two decades, food consumption has also increased. While some 733 million people in the region still live in absolute poverty and 537 million are undernourished, average consumption has risen from 2,379 kilocalories per capita per day in 1990 to 2,665 in 2009.[140] A large number of Asians are enjoying a much richer diet than has been the case historically. In 1982, an average Chinese person consumed only 13 kilos of meat per year; the Chinese now eat four times as much and consume a quarter of the world's meat supply (71 million tonnes a year).[141]

[136] Gaurav Moghe, 'India Communists: Naxalite Rebels Are Country's Greatest Internal Threat', Policy Mic, 26 May 2013, www.policymic.com/articles/44649/india-communists-naxalite-rebels-are-country-s-greatest-internal-threat.

[137] SIPRI, 'Military Expenditure' as of February 2014, http://portal.sipri.org/publications/pages/expenditures/country-search.

[138] Qatar Foundation, 'New Harvests in the Desert', 19 September 2013, http://www.qf.org.qa/page?a=832&lang=en-CA.

[139] Emiko Terazono, Jack Farchy and Roman Olearchyk, 'Ukraine bans wheat exports', Financial Times, 19 October 2012, http://www.ft.com/cms/s/0/153a6fc2-19db-11e2-a379-00144feabdc0.html?siteedition=uk#axzz2uVzsuPMX.

[140] Asian Development Bank, 'Food Security in Africa', August 2013, www.adb.org/publications/food-security-asia-and-pacific.

[141] Malcom Moore, 'China now eats twice as much meat as the United States', Daily Telegraph, 12 October 2012, www.telegraph.co.uk/news/worldnews/asia/china/9605048/China-now-eats-twice-as-much-meat-as-the-United-States.html.

Some efforts are being made to respond to scarcity with the creation of food banks.[142] However, without a coordinated response, in the longer term it is likely that factors such as increasing populations, climate change and migration will lead to more price shocks and greater food insecurity.

Of the countries considered in this report, Indonesia is the most concerned about the possibility of rising food insecurity and the possible implications for its broader security; in part this is due to its focus on self-sufficiency and on internal threats. It is acutely aware that unless it can gain more control over its food requirements it will remain susceptible to outside pressure and constraints. Perhaps surprisingly, despite its small size and therefore high dependence on outsiders for meeting its food needs, this is not a concern expressed by Singapore. Nor is it among Indian policy-makers despite the problems that country experienced during the food-price spikes in recent years (and its high poverty levels). This is probably due to more immediate traditional security threats (i.e. Pakistan, insurgency, terrorism).

Water

According to a 2012 Chatham House report, 'freshwater scarcity presents one of the most pressing cross-cutting challenges for our resources futures'.[143] Some scenarios show that global demand for water already exceeds sustainable supply and this could worsen in the coming decades. An estimated 80% of the world's population lives in areas with a high threat of water scarcity. This not only threatens the population directly but has concrete impacts also on economic growth, from agriculture to energy, industry and mineral extraction.

Several of the areas where the threat of water scarcity is particularly acute are in Asia: Kashmir, Vietnam, India and Pakistan. China also faces growing scarcity in the north of the country and this is likely to worsen as demand increases both nationally and regionally. Even highly developed Singapore is affected, dependent as it is on water imports from Malaysia.[144] Some countries, such as India, have seen significant falls in their groundwater tables owing to over-consumption (Delhi has suffered notable decreases), which may be encouraged by subsidies: unless significant action is taken this will only

get worse in the coming decades.[145] There are multiple potential repercussions from major internal migration leading to internal conflict and instability, to intrastate conflict when, for example, communal transboundary rivers are dammed.

Water is also increasingly being used as an instrument of leverage between states. The ongoing negotiations and arbitration by the World Bank between India and Pakistan over the Baglihar Dam continues to be a source of conflict despite the Indus Waters Treaty, ratified in 1960, which many hold to be one of the more successful of such treaties. Similar tensions over water are present in other parts of South and Southeast Asia.

By 2050, three-quarters of world's population could face acute freshwater scarcity. Competition for water resources will only escalate along with 'competition between resource production and other societal uses'.[146] With its large population and rapidly growing economies, the future of the Asia-Pacific region will be tied to the availability and security of water.

Minerals

As mentioned above, China halted the export of rare-earth minerals to Japan in 2010 as a punishment and a source of ongoing leverage for what it perceived to be Japanese intransigence over the arrest of a Chinese fishing boat captain. At that time, China controlled 97% of the world's resources of such minerals; stopping exports thus had significant implications for a number of Japanese manufacturers (including of weapons).[147] The action appeared to have the desired effect, leading Japan to release the captain and to be perhaps more wary of further antagonizing China. Japan and South Korea are particularly sensitive to such measures as they are heavily reliant on rare-earth minerals and metal imports for many of their high-tech industries.

It appears likely that China and others will continue to use these instruments for leverage, particularly when they control a majority of the resources concerned. However, such levers can sometimes have short life-spans. Following China's actions, a number of other countries, most notably Australia and Malaysia, started to build mining operations for the same minerals, which will, in time, diminish

[142] 'South Asia: Regional food bank gets go-ahead', Irin, 7 August 2008, www.irinnews.org/report/79689/south-asia-regional-food-bank-gets-go-ahead.

[143] Bernice Lee, Felix Preston, Jaakko Kooroshy, Rob Bailey and Glada Lahn, *Resources Futures*, Chatham House Report, December 2012, http://www.chathamhouse.org/publications/papers/view/187947, p. 67. For a detailed study on the situation in South Asia, see Gareth Price (ed.), *Attitudes to Water in South Asia* (Chatham House, forthcoming May 2014).

[144] Anges Teh, 'Resource scarcity drives Singapore to sustainability leadership', Bloomberg News, 22 January 2013, www.bloomberg.com/news/2013-01-22/resource-scarcity-drives-singapore-to-sustainability-leadership.html.

[145] 'Delhi worst hit by water shortage: Survey', *Economic Times*, 25 December 2013, http://articles.economictimes.indiatimes.com/2013-12-25/news/45561586_1_rural-households-water-shortage-aam-aadmi-party.

[146] Lee et al., *Resources Futures*, p. 69.

[147] Ambrose Evans-Pritchard, 'Japan breaks China's stranglehold on rare metals with sea-mud bonanza', *Daily Telegraph*, 24 March 2013, www.telegraph.co.uk/finance/comment/ambroseevans_pritchard/9951299/Japan-breaks-Chinas-stranglehold-on-rare-metals-with-sea-mud-bonanza.html.

China's hold over the industry and weaken its ability to attempt similar pressure in the future. Furthermore, Japan discovered potentially game-changing deposits of rare-earth minerals in its waters in March 2013.[148]

Nevertheless, restricting the flow of such materials as well as other natural resources will continue to be instruments of power used by resource-rich countries.

Fossil fuels and energy

Energy security, and in particular securing sufficient fossil fuels, will be a top concern for countries across Asia (as elsewhere) in the coming decades and therefore a point of pressure. From 2000 to 2010, the share of global fossil fuels going to China and India doubled in value terms (4.4% to 10.8%) and more than tripled in weight terms (4.5% to 14.3%). Consumption in India and Indonesia in particular (of the countries covered here) is likely to grow further as they follow the same path taken by more affluent economies such as South Korea and Japan. Unless domestic production of unconventional energy sources significantly exceeds current expectations, import dependence will only increase, leading to further reliance on energy-exporting regions, including the Middle East, Russia, West Africa, Australia and possibly East Africa.[149]

Given projected consumption increases, the countries considered here will need to pursue a variety of mechanisms to ensure diversification and mitigate risk. Many would like to increase the share of natural gas. How to do this is not clear, however; it is unlikely that the American shale gas 'revolution' could be replicated in Asia, and access to other sources such as those in Russia, Bangladesh, Burma (Myanmar) and Iran will require extremely complex and difficult negotiations over pipelines and prices.[150] Renewable energy could also provide some extra protection. Significant progress has been made in some parts of Asia with regard to renewables, particularly hydropower. However, it remains a very small part of total production (for example, Japan's renewables only account for around 6% of total energy consumption).[151] Strategic reserves may provide some countries with a buffer against external pressure on energy resources. However, few of the countries considered in this study have any reserves (India alone has started to build a significant stockpile of oil).[152]

India will be particularly susceptible to pressure over energy. It is anticipated that it could surpass China on energy consumption; and it is already expected to overtake China in coal imports in the 2020s.[153] Japan, while not seeing the demand growth faced by many others, is also vulnerable, particularly following the shutdown in 2012 of its nuclear reactors, which until then had met 30% of its energy needs. The country is now even more heavily dependent on energy imports, meeting less than 15% of its demand domestically. Japan ranks as the world's largest liquefied natural gas importer, second largest coal importer and third largest net oil importer.[154]

Figure 4: Projected Asia-Pacific energy consumption

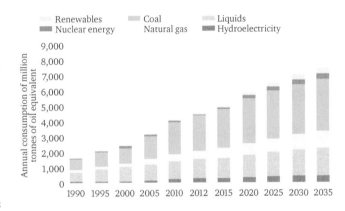

Source: BP Energy Outlook 2035, http://www.bp.com/en/global/corporate/about-bp/energy-economics/energy-outlook.html.

In addition to tensions over access to external energy resources, potential sources internal to the Asia-Pacific region could be an even more direct cause of conflict. In theory, large oil and gas resources located underneath the South and East China Seas could prove useful in meeting growing Asian energy demand. However, given that the waters and reserves are disputed, including in the East China Sea by China, Japan, South Korea, Taiwan, and in the South China Sea by China, Vietnam, Malaysia, Taiwan, the Philippines, Indonesia and Brunei, accessing these reserves may increase rather than lessen tensions. Either way it is politically unfeasible to extract them in the medium term.

---

[148] Ibid.

[149] Lee et al., *Resources Futures*, p. 24.

[150] According to Martin Houston, chief operating officer and executive director of the BG Group, the pace and scale of the shale gas revolution in North America 'will not and probably cannot be replicated in the foreseeable future'. Chico Harlan, 'Asia wants a piece of US shale gas boom; Japan, South Korea seek lower-cost LNG', *Washington Post*, 15 October 2013, www.washingtonpost.com/world/asia-wants-a-piece-of-us-shale-gas-boom-japan-south-korea-seek-lower-cost-lng/2013/10/15/ac161cb8-359e-11e3-89db-8002ba99b894_story_1.html.

[151] US Energy Information Administration, 'Japan', 29 October 2013, http://www.eia.gov/countries/cab.cfm?fips=JA, and US Energy Information Administration, 'China', 4 February 2014, www.eia.gov/countries/cab.cfm?fips=CH.

[152] Lee et al., *Resources Futures*, p. 95.

[153] Ibid., p. 25.

[154] US Energy Information Administration, 'Japan: Overview', 29 October 2013, www.eia.gov/countries/cab.cfm?fips=JA.

Cyber insecurity

Cyber-attacks have been prevalent for a number of years, either alone or as a prelude to a broader conflict. In 2008, at the start of their war over South Ossetia, Russia was accused of conducting a major cyber-attack on Georgia. The United States and Israel have allegedly used cyber-attacks (Stuxnet in 2010 and Flash in 2012) against Iran's nuclear weapons programme. As the February 2013 Mandiant report made clear, and as the Pentagon's 'Annual Report to Congress' in May 2013 reiterated,

> In 2012, numerous computer systems around the world, including those owned by the U.S. government, continued to be targeted for intrusions, some of which appear to be attributable directly to the Chinese government and military.[155]

North Korea was accused of conducting cyber-attacks on South Korean banks and other infrastructure during the 2013 crisis.[156]

These kinds of attacks, along with hacking to find and exploit loopholes and gaps in security for future use, are all clear threats to the countries in the Asia-Pacific region. While it appears that China holds the greatest capabilities in this respect, other countries in the region, including India, Japan, North Korea and South Korea, are increasingly building similar capacity. Many countries are also beginning to build up the capacity to defend themselves against such threats.

Given their low cost and the low barriers to entry, in recent years there has been a rise in the number of cyber-attacks led, apparently, by hacker groups or individuals targeting governments or other entities.

Cyber espionage is another threat. Increasingly it appears that state and non-state actors are hacking into private organizations and other governments. This can be a direct security threat – when they hack and gain access to military technologies or diplomatic secrets – as well as a more non-traditional one, for example when they take advantage of stolen industrial secrets, thereby affecting a company's bottom line. These threats have both security and economic implications.

Given their low cost and the low barriers to entry (in terms of hardware and software), in recent years there has been a rise in the number of cyber-attacks led, apparently, by hacker groups or individuals targeting governments or other entities. These groups have engaged in activities ranging from relatively simple denial-of-service attacks to more complex operations that have brought down web servers or damaged systems. As in the case of the 2012 attack on oil producer Saudi Aramco's computer system when a virus infected about 30,000 of its workstations, it was unclear whether the instigators were a state (allegedly Iran) or a non-state agent (a group called 'Cutting Sword of Justice' claimed responsibility online).[157] It will remain difficult to assign blame for such attacks and thus put in place appropriate deterrents.

Space insecurity

On 11 January 2007, China conducted an anti-satellite missile test by blowing up one of its own weather satellites. With this act it joined the United States and Russia as the only countries with the capability to destroy a satellite in space. Given the dependence of many militaries on satellite technology, not least that of the United States, this is a significant point of leverage to which the Chinese military now has access.

Following the successful test, China announced that it had no intention of embarking on 'any kind of arms race in outer space', and it continues to insist that it wants space to remain a peaceful arena.[158] It has participated in a number of efforts to reach international agreement on a code of conduct in space. In fact, until January 2012 when Secretary of State Hillary Clinton announced that United States had 'decided to join with the European Union and other nations to develop an International Code of Conduct for Outer Space Activities', it was Washington that was proving to be the obstacle to progress on this front.[159] Nevertheless, China has sent a clear message to any power that is using space-based technologies that it has the capacity to destroy their satellites.

[155] US Department of Defense, 'Annual Report to Congress: Military and Security Developments Involving the People's Republic of China 2013', 6 May 2013, www.defense.gov/pubs/2013_china_report_final.pdf. See also Andrew S. Erickson, 'Pentagon Report Reveals Chinese Military Developments', *The Diplomat*, 8 March 2013, http://thediplomat.com/2013/05/back-on-track-pentagon-report-reveals-chinese-military-developments/; Mandiant, 'Mandiant releases report exposing one of china's cyber espionage groups', https://www.mandiant.com/news/release/mandiant-releases-report-exposing-one-of-chinas-cyber-espionage-groups/.

[156] 'South Korea blames North for bank and TV cyber-attacks', BBC News, 10 April 2013, www.bbc.co.uk/news/technology-22092051.

[157] Daniel Fineren and Amena Bakr, 'Saudi Aramco says most damage from computer attack fixed', Reuters, 26 August 2012, www.reuters.com/article/2012/08/26/net-us-saudi-aramco-hacking-idUSBRE87P0B020120826.

[158] Joseph Kahn, 'China Shows Assertiveness in Weapons Test', *New York Times*, 20 January 2007. www.nytimes.com/2007/01/20/world/asia/20china.html?ex=15768 0000&en=515b27578ee57de2&ei=5124&partner=permalink&exprod=permalink&_r=0.

[159] US Department of State, 'International Code of Conduct for Outer Space Activities', 17 January 2012, www.state.gov/secretary/20092013clinton/rm/2012/01/180969.htm.

Economic insecurity

The final tool, principally used by states, that many in the region consider to be a significant source of threat is economic leverage. As noted above, this concern is particularly acute in relation to China. Given the economic dependence of many countries in the region on China, its ability to cut off trade or investment would enable it to have a significant impact on the abilities of these countries to maintain growth and meet the needs of their populations. This can be used both as a threat and as a coercive tool.

In response to this perceived dependence on China, many countries in the region are increasingly trying to diversify their investments and their trade partners. Until recently, many of them looked to India, among others, to provide an alternative. However, as India's economy has stagnated, and corruption and bureaucracy have raised the cost of doing business there, China has become again the principal driver of economic growth in the region. Given its population, it is unlikely that this trend towards dependence on China will be reversed in the near term (even in the event of a future major Chinese downturn). As stated above, countries such as Australia, Japan and South Korea feel themselves particularly susceptible to threats of this kind.

4. Responses

There are three principal avenues for the states considered in this report to meet the threats and challenges listed above. They can:

- strengthen their domestic capabilities;

- reach out to and partner with other countries in the region through formal or informal engagement (through regional and plurilateral organizations[160]); and

- look to the United States (as has historically been the case) to help strengthen and reinforce their capabilities.

While the first of these might be considered the initial port of call and is one that many of them are actively pursuing, no country (including the United States) will be able to meet its security needs alone, given the variety of threats. Building domestic capabilities also takes a long time and thus is not a solution in the short to medium term. Thus the focus of this chapter is on the viability and alternatives of the last two options (both of which are likely to be needed).

The role of regional partnerships and alliances

In recent years there has been a proliferation of groupings in the Asia-Pacific region. The main ones now are the Shanghai Cooperation Organization (SCO), the East Asia Summit (EAS), Asia-Pacific Economic Cooperation (APEC), the Association of South East Asian Nations (ASEAN) and the multiple adjunct groups to the latter including ASEAN+1, ASEAN+3, the ASEAN Regional Forum (ARF), the ASEAN Defence Ministers Meeting (ADMM) and ASEAN Defence Ministers Meeting-Plus (ADMM+), all of which have vague and overlapping roles and responsibilities. The variety among the membership has a significant influence on their objectives, activities and intent. For example, the membership of the ARF, which includes India and Pakistan, has different capacities and opportunities for impact from the EAS, and this in turn has different possibilities from ASEAN, which does not include China and the United States.

In addition to these regional groups, there has also been an upsurge in the number of regional bilateral, trilateral and plurilateral groups in the past decade. The countries that have been more actively engaged in such initiatives include Australia, Japan and India. These more informal, ad hoc groups can provide a launching pad for initiatives that subsequently move to, and are subsumed within, the larger formal groups. But when progress is impossible in these larger groups (which are often driven by consensus), the smaller ones can sometimes take action instead.

The opportunities for and obstacles to engaging through these regional and plurilateral groups are discussed below.

The value added of regional groups

Regional partnerships and alliances have the potential to play an important role in mitigating the threats discussed above. They all, either formally or by tradition, make decisions by consensus. As such, the objectives of each tend towards often vague and ambiguous language that is open to interpretation (and therefore can be agreed upon). They also tend towards the lowest common denominator for action. It is the differences in the margins that often prevent a more assertive role for these organizations, particularly those with larger, more diverse memberships. As such, they have often been criticized by outsiders as being ineffective or impotent. In comparison with other regional groups such as NATO and the EU, to external actors in the West these Asia-Pacific bodies seem inadequate for the weighty tasks their members face.

Despite these criticisms, their members see them as important entities with tangible and concrete objectives and roles. Even the more security-related organizations such as the EAS, and the various ASEAN entities, which are focused on potentially the most sensitive issues with the greatest diversity of opinion around the region, offer a number of clear benefits. Some of their major challenges and opportunities are outlined below.

Networks and facilitation

One of the principal functions of the established regional organizations is to facilitate discussion and, where possible, resolve issues of contention. In the six countries in this study, their ability to explore and consider sensitive issues through regular meetings, thus providing opportunities for the resolution of difficult problems and disagreements, is highly rated (even though it is recognized that agreement is hard to reach).

Navigation of the sea lanes in the South and East China Seas, a highly sensitive topic for many in the region, is one example frequently given of the value of these regional bodies. Despite the inability to achieve a resolution of related disputes, the fact that they can be raised in these forums represents progress in the minds of many. The failure of the 2012 ASEAN foreign ministers' meeting to agree a final joint statement has been highlighted by some as an example of a success: the mere fact that it could be discussed and that China felt the need to block the statement shows the relevance of the group. The members are investing notable resources in these organizations.

---

[160] 'Plurilateral' is used to describe smaller multilateral organizations, without a mandated regional basis, that focus on particular issues or relationships. These can range from trilateral groups to those with a much broader, but not entirely inclusive, membership.

In addition to facilitation, more broadly these forums develop a network of relationships that provide a web of infrastructure and engagement, which is played out in their regular meetings. In some instances, these have expanded to encompass the establishment of working groups that share best practices and lessons about technical security issues such as de-mining, humanitarian assistance and disaster response. Such loose but sticky lines of communication create a flexible but nevertheless strong set of connections between various parties that they are loath to break. The benefits are intangible but important.

Training and capacity-building

Regional groups also provide substantive opportunities for collective training and capacity-building, and an opportunity for the member states to swap lessons learned. For example, the ADMM+ has five working groups – on humanitarian assistance and disaster relief, maritime security, military medicine, counter-terrorism and peace-keeping operations – through which members are able to exchange experiences and potentially share resources and facilitate collaboration. A high-profile example of this was a humanitarian intervention and disaster-relief (HADR)/ military medicine joint exercise in June 2013 encompassing more than 3,000 troops from 18 countries including the United States, China, Japan, India and Indonesia.[161] In September 2013, ADMM+ members held joint counter-terrorism training exercises.[162] Such training also takes place through other organizations, such as ASEAN itself. In 2013, Indonesia hosted an ASEAN-sponsored counter-terrorism joint training exercise in which member states shared best practice.[163]

While training and capacity-building are an important resource provided by these regional organizations, this is often seen as insufficient to meet the challenges. Despite working together on HADR activities, ASEAN was criticized for its slow and inadequate response to the typhoon that hit the Philippines in November 2013. While countries such as Thailand and Singapore dispatched vital support bilaterally, ASEAN played a minimal role in coordinating these efforts.[164] While these activities are important, there are significant opportunities to do more.

Norm-building

Finally, these regional organizations provide a useful venue in which norms and regional consensus can be built. Creating norms, whether with regard to definitions of terrorism or informal agreement on laws of the sea, plays a vital role in providing guidelines for all regional actors and in lowering the risk that misunderstanding or mismanagement could lead to tensions and potentially conflict. As such, norms are inevitably easier to realize through organizations whose membership has common interests; ASEAN and the SCO (to name two) have been more successful in these initiatives than the groups with more diverse membership such as the EAS.

The value of plurilateral groups

The rise of plurilateral groups is relatively recent, following the creation of a plethora of new dialogues and informal partnerships. As mentioned above, the principal protagonists in the region include India, Australia and Japan.

Australia's motivation probably stems in large part from its unique location in Asia – its distance from any other actors leaves it isolated and potentially vulnerable, in particular to any changes in maritime connectivity and openness – and from demographic trends that will increasingly make migration (most likely from Asia) a vital strategy to maintain growth.[165] Thus it needs to cover significant territory with limited resources. As for Japan, the restrictions its constitution imposes on the Self-Defense Forces, while now in a state of flux, have arguably made it more open in recent years to closer engagement with other regional powers. India's rise has made it a more attractive partner to others, particularly to those that want to retain flexibility and choice in their foreign policy and not be beholden to bigger powers.

Over the past 10 years, Japan has launched trilateral strategic dialogues with the United States and, respectively, India and Australia. The US–Japan–Australia Trilateral Strategic Dialogue (TSD) was launched at 'senior officials' level in 2002, and elevated to foreign ministers' level in 2006, while the US–Japan–India trilateral first met officially in 2011.[166] An India–Australia–US trilateral was also launched in 2011 although it appears to have made little

---

[161] Michito Tsuruoka, 'PacNet #69 – An Era of the ADMM-Plus? Unique Achievements and Challenges', Center for Strategic International Studies, 5 September 2013, http://csis.org/publication/pacnet-69-era-admm-plus-unique-achievements-and-challenges.

[162] Atho' Ullah, 'Joint counter terrorism training exercise given green light', Demotix, 9 September 2013, www.demotix.com/news/2629190/joint-counter-terrorism-training-exercise-given-green-light#media-2628921.

[163] Ibid.

[164] Euan Graham, 'PacNet #82 – Abenomics and Japan's Defense Priorities', Center for Strategic International Studies, 5 November 2013, https://csis.org/files/publication/Pac1382.pdf.

[165] This latter issue, migration, is a hugely controversial one and it not yet being openly discussed.

[166] US Department of State, 'US-Japan-India Trilateral', 19 December 2011, www.state.gov/r/pa/prs/ps/2011/12/179172.htm.

progress since. In 2007, for a brief period, a 'Quadrilateral Security Dialogue' was posited between Japan, the United States, Australia and India. However, fears expressed by some of the actors that China would see this as an attempt to encircle it led to the idea being quickly dropped. All of these informal groups, while focusing strongly on security issues, have made it clear that they should not be seen as efforts to 'counter China'.

It is not only these four main players that have been involved in trilateral or plurilateral groups. Perhaps one of the most potentially interesting combinations was the creation in 2008 of a trilateral group by China, Japan and South Korea. Since its launch this has undergone ups and downs, enormously influenced by the broader context between the three. However, even during periods of great diplomatic turmoil, this trilateral has not been shut down (although some meetings have been cancelled). One of the principal goals of the group is a free trade agreement, although discussion on security and geopolitical issues also takes place.[167]

These plurilaterals often fill the gaps left by the larger, more formal regional groups. Many of the challenges that the latter face can be addressed to some extent by these more informal and flexible partnerships. Some of their principal benefits are as follows.

Generating agreement and building momentum

Not unlike the formal groups, the plurilaterals provide a forum where states with similar views can explore and, where possible, find agreement on sensitive issues. In particular, when the regional groups find it impossible to reach consensus owing to their wider membership, these smaller informal groups can be more effective in implementing action. This is particularly the case when some of the bigger players, such as the United States, China, India and Japan are involved, which can make finding common ground particularly complex and difficult.

These groups are also effective venues for developing ideas and building momentum on issues which the regional groups find hard to tackle. Once such momentum has been created, the members of the plurilateral group can take their ideas to the larger groups to develop them into broader initiatives. The inherent informality of the plurilaterals and their greater confidentiality (unlike the formal regional groups, they tend not to produce joint statements) provide greater opportunity for their members to float new ideas at a relatively low cost diplomatically, politically and with their publics. Their ad hoc nature ensures that they avoid the sensitivities that agreements in formal groups would raise.

Success in these plurilaterals is not necessarily measured by reaching agreement on an issue, but instead by building relationships between a smaller number of states or by merely raising and discussing sensitive topics in a relatively private setting, so potentially avoiding a more public (and potentially kinetic) action. For example, while the China–Japan–South Korea trilateral has seen only very halting progress since its launch, it does provide an ongoing (albeit irregular) opportunity for the three, whose relations are often very tense and delicate, to explore areas of potential commonality and find diplomatic ways to address challenges. At the other end of the spectrum, the US–India–Japan trilateral, encompassing countries with quite similar interests, are more likely to make concrete progress on issues and take bigger steps in advancing common understanding.

Facilitating joint training and operations, and capacity-building

The plurilateral groups are also effective venues for conducting joint training and exercises. In many cases these exercises eventually expand beyond the original players to encompass a far wider array of regional and, potentially, super-regional actors. For example, in 2012 the United States undertook training exercises with Australia, Thailand, Malaysia and Indonesia.[168] In 2007, the United States, Japan, India, Singapore and Australia held joint military exercises.[169] Such exercises and training, when combined with the strategic dialogues through which these plurilateral groups engage, provide a more effective basis for joint operations.

Some of the least controversial and most effective cases of this are in the area of humanitarian assistance and disaster relief. Anti-piracy initiatives also benefit from the platform provided by the plurilaterals. Freedom of navigation and maritime security were important agenda items for meetings between foreign ministers and defence ministers as part of the US–Japan–Australia Trilateral in 2013, and all three countries have been involved in the anti-piracy efforts, signing an Anti-Counterfeiting Trade Agreement in 2011 (although these efforts were not officially coordinated).[170]

---

[167] In a joint declaration released at the Trilateral Summit in 2012, the three countries listed 'enhancing mutual political trust, deepening economic and trade cooperation, promoting sustainable development and strengthening communication and coordination' as priorities for future cooperation. Xiaolei Gu, 'China-Japan-South Korea Sign Trilateral Agreement and Launch FTA Talks', China Briefing, 14 May 2012, www.china-briefing.com/news/2012/05/14/china-japan-south-korea-sign-trilateral-agreement-and-launch-fta-talks.html.

[168] Elisabeth Bumiller, 'Words and deeds show focus of the American military on Asia', New York Times, 10 November 2012, www.nytimes.com/2012/11/11/world/asia/us-militarys-new-focus-on-asia-becomes-clearer.html?pagewanted=1&_r=0.

[169] 'Exercise Malabar 07-2 Kicks Off', America's Navy, 9 July 2007, http://www.navy.mil/submit/display.asp?story_id=31691.

[170] J. Berkshire Miller, 'US-Japan-Australia: A Trilateral With Purpose?', The Diplomat, 25 October 2013, http://thediplomat.com/2013/10/u-s-japan-australia-a-trilateral-with-purpose/?allpages=yes.

Finally, as with the regional groups, the plurilaterals assist in capacity-building. For example, in 2003 Malaysia created the Southeast Asia Regional Center for Counter-terrorism, which brings together training and capacity-building for a number of countries and partners in the region. Where some countries have more capacity and capability than others, such initiatives are a way of broadening the assets and learning from one another.

The gaps that partnerships cannot fill

The different groups in the Asia-Pacific region have limitations. Unlike NATO or the EU, neither the formal regional groups nor the informal plurilaterals are action-oriented (the former in particular). They do not have mechanisms for coming together either to sanction or to create joint operations against an external or internal threat. Nor should they, in the view of their membership; many Asian countries are deeply sceptical about whether Europe's deep multinational integration can or should be applied in Asia. In recent years they have been dismissive of the EU and NATO, not least given current questions regarding these institutions' long-term role and effectiveness.

In fact, the lack of operationalization in Asia-Pacific regional bodies is intentional on the part of the participants. Few desire a more active, engaged group that would limit their sovereignty. Given the relatively recent independence of a number of the states concerned (particularly in Southeast Asia) and the still strong memories of conflict between them, the primacy of sovereignty is paramount.[171] This is particularly true in the case of the formal groups.

> In fact, the lack of operationalization in Asia-Pacific regional bodies is intentional on the part of the participants. Few desire a more active, engaged group that would limit their sovereignty.

Member states would also find it extremely hard to participate in a more actively operational and formal organization. Given their disparity of interests and differences in perceptions of threats (as laid out in the previous chapter), it would be impossible for the members, particularly in the larger groups, to reach consensus on action in all but the most benign or extreme cases. This is less problematic in the informal groups, whose members typically have more closely aligned interests and perspectives.

At the same time, some would like to see a stronger role for certain regional groups. As stated above, ASEAN is a central element of Indonesia's foreign policy. Singapore is also very keen to see a stronger role for Indonesia in ASEAN and is quietly supporting such a move. However, it is unlikely that many of the other Southeast Asian member states are looking for a stronger ASEAN and it is hard to conceive what more assertive actions the organization would be able to agree upon.

The role of the United States

Since President Obama's announcement of the rebalance in 2011, the United States has worked to reassure its allies in the region of its continued engagement, to dissuade them from too assertive actions and to deter potential threats. The increase in military assets, heavy emphasis on the Trans-Pacific Partnership (TPP – a proposed trade agreement including many in the region) and strong diplomatic engagement have emphasized America's intention to remain an Asia-Pacific power and to sustain its presence and engagement in the region.[172]

However, as this report makes clear, America's role in the region is dictated not just by its own desires, but by those of its regional partners and by broader contextual dynamics that can restrict or expand its reach and capabilities. These three aspects – context, regional desire and US interests – will also dictate how America's regional role will change in the future.

Contextual changes

As its Asia-Pacific friends and partners consider what they want from the United States, it is vital to understand the broader contextual constraints that are affecting America's capabilities and actions. There are a number of broad changes taking place within and outside the United States that will influence its role in the region in the coming years and decades.

America's budget constraints
The ability of the United States to project power abroad is in part determined by the vitality of its economy. While this has been a traditional strength, in recent years economic factors have become a liability. Although it has returned to steady growth, the United States continues to face a difficult long-term fiscal situation owing to factors ranging from the national debt, growth in entitlements spending, the continuing fallout from the global financial crisis and

---

[171] Joshua Kurlantzick, *ASEAN's Future and Asian Integration*, Center for Strategic and International Studies, November 2012.

[172] TPP partner countries include Australia, Brunei, Chile, Canada, Japan, Malaysia, Mexico, New Zealand, Peru, Singapore, the United States and Vietnam. In addition, Taiwan and South Korea have announced their interest in joining.

a lack of political consensus on tackling these problems. Despite some recent good economic news, such as the energy revolution, declining unemployment (down to 6.7%) and a shrinking budget deficit, the United States has a number of structural and political challenges it still needs to overcome.[173]

Political polarization in Washington has made addressing short-term problems extremely hard and prevented a serious discussion of longer-term problems from taking place. It has even resulted in some self-inflicted wounds, such as sequestration, which has led to defence cuts of almost $500 billion over the next 10 years (coming on top of the cuts of $487 billion from defence spending over 10 years, announced in 2011).[174] While many in the United States are in favour of reducing defence expenditure, very few are happy with the way the sequester mechanism enacts these cuts. The federal budget that was agreed in January does take some steps to mitigate the worst impact of sequestration on defence, but much of the burden remains (for example, in 2013 it led to civilian furloughs in the Department of Defense).

Figure 5 demonstrates the path US defence spending may take and highlights the remaining uncertainty surrounding it. According to the Congressional Budget Office (CBO), expenditure is likely to follow modest or no growth in the coming years (if spending for contingency operations in Iraq and Afghanistan is excluded). What the diagram does not illustrate, however, is how cuts will tangibly affect the various forces. The army is likely to be most affected, with the active force potentially decreasing to 440,000, its lowest level since before the Second World War. According to the latest budget laid out by Secretary Hagel in February, while the Marines will have to shrink (to 182,000), Special Forces will increase by 4,000.[175] There will also be cuts in equipment from fighter planes to the proposed cancellation of the Ground Combat Vehicle Program and, if more is needed, the mothballing of the aircraft carrier *USS George Washington* (for which repairs are currently on hold).[176] The navy has reduced by half its order of F-35s over the next five years and plans for more littoral combat ships have been put on hold. Other areas, notably cyber security, unmanned aerial vehicles, and research and development,

Figure 5: Cost of Department of Defense's plans

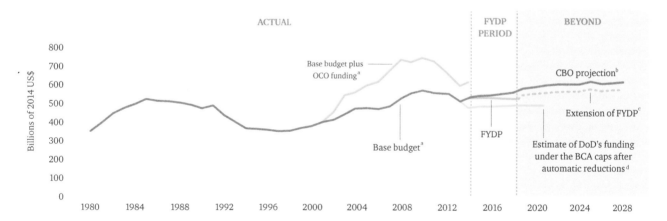

Source: Congressional Budget Office.
Note: FYDP = Future Years Defense Program; FYDP period = 2014–18, the years for which the Department of Defense's (DoD) plans are fully specified.
a. For 2002–14, supplemental and emergency funding for overseas contingency operations (OCO), such as those in Afghanistan and Iraq, and for other purposes is shown separately from the base-budget data.
b. The CBO projection of the base budget incorporates costs that are consistent with Department of Defense's recent experience.
c. For the extension of the FYDP from 2019 to 2032, CBO projects the costs of the Department of Defense's plans using the department's estimates of costs to the extent they are available and costs that are consistent with CBO's projections of price and compensation trends in the overall economy where the department's estimates are not available.
d. Base-budget data include supplemental and emergency funding before 2002.

[173] US Department of Labor, Bureau of Labor Statistics, 'Labor Force Statistics from the Current Population Survey', February 2014, http://data.bls.gov/timeseries/LNS14000000; and David Lawder, 'US deficit to decline, then rise as labor market struggles: CBO', Reuters, 4 February 2014, http://www.reuters.com/article/2014/02/04/us-usa-fiscal-idUSBREA1308920140204.
[174] Congress Budget Office, 'Estimated Impact of Automatic Budget Enforcement Procedures Specified in the Budget Control Act', 12 September 2011, www.cbo.gov/publication/42754; Lawrence J. Korb, Alex Rothman, and Max Hoffman, '$100 Billion in Politically Feasible Defense Cuts for a Budget Deal', Centre for American Progress, 6 December 2012, www.americanprogress.org/issues/military/report/2012/12/06/47106/hundred-billion-in-politically-feasible-defense-cuts-for-a-budget-deal/; and US Department of Defense, 'Defense Budget: Priorities and Choices', January 2012, http://www.defense.gov/news/Defense_Budget_Priorities.pdf.
[175] Nick Simeone, 'Hagel Outlines Budget Reducing Troop Strength, Force Structure', US Department of Defense, http://www.defense.gov/news/newsarticle.aspx?id=121703.
[176] Zachary Keck, 'US Navy Faces Aircraft Carrier Cuts', *The Diplomat*, 29 January 2014, http://thediplomat.com/2014/01/us-navy-faces-aircraft-carrier-cuts/.

have been protected or seen funding increases.[177] However, over the longer term, personnel costs (currently 46% of total spending for the Army) are set to increase across the military despite the reduction in troop levels (consequently squeezing other areas of the budget over time).[178]

It is in this context that the new 60:40 balance of assets towards the Pacific must be understood. Budget restrictions will mean that, while the ratio of forces changes, the total number of forces in the Asia-Pacific region will not necessarily increase and may in time even decrease. The impact will be felt not just in the military arena but also possibly in terms of economic and diplomatic engagement, and development assistance.

America's inward vision
During his 2012 re-election campaign and in his 2013 inaugural speech President Obama alluded to the theme of 'nation-building at home'.[179] This was a reflection of an increasing American desire to be less involved in foreign adventures and more focused on a growing list of domestic challenges. This new attitude is not restricted to Obama, nor to the Democratic Party – it can also be seen in the growing popularity of more isolationist Republican politicians, such as Senator Rand Paul. A new attitude can also be detected among influential American foreign-policy thinkers such as Richard Haass, in his 2013 book *Foreign Policy Begins at Home* (although it should be stressed he argues against isolationism).

The political and policy transition towards a less engaged America is supported by public opinion.[180] According to a Pew Research survey, conducted immediately after the elections, 83% of Americans thought the president should focus on domestic policy and only 6% that he should focus on foreign policy.[181] Just over half of Americans (51%) believed the United States is over-extended abroad, according to polling in 2013. A similar portion (52%) agreed that it 'should mind its own business internationally and let other countries get along the best they can on their own'.[182]

In many regards Americans are keen to move away from the role of 'world's policeman' and are hoping that other countries will bear some of the burden of maintaining global stability.

A move away from international engagement may also be facilitated by several domestic factors. The US energy revolution has driven some commentators to argue that America can afford to extract itself from commitments in the Middle East and elsewhere. Improvements in food production and a return of some manufacturing to the United States have also helped develop the case that the country is regaining some independence. The counter-arguments – that globalization has ensured greater global interdependence than ever and that the United States will never be able to cut itself off from the rest of the world, whether in energy terms or economically – appear to have less resonance with the public.

> According to a Pew Research survey, conducted immediately after the elections, 83% of Americans thought the president should focus on domestic policy and only 6% that he should focus on foreign policy.

The fallout of the Iraq and Afghanistan wars is still palpable in the US political system. It is worth remembering that President Obama was elected in 2008 with a clear record of opposition to the 2003 Iraq war and re-elected in 2012 having promised to bring troops home from Afghanistan. After these and the Libyan intervention, there is a feeling among Americans that in the Middle East 'even well-intended interventions don't work out'.[183] The 2013 debate over Syria also showed consistent public scepticism about the merits of intervention.

Another consequence of the recent military engagements in the Middle East is that it will be increasingly difficult for US leaders to pursue new wars in areas that have no obvious strategic interest for the United States. This perception is leading a number of Asian allies to question more than ever whether it would come to their aid in a territorial conflict in the region. Under these circumstances, it will take strong leadership by an American president to convince the US public of the strategic necessity of military action.

[177] Marcus Weisgerber, 'QDR Emphasizes Cyber, Science and Technology', *Defense News*, 4 March 2014, http://www.defensenews.com/article/20140304/DEFREG02/303040038/QDR-Emphasizes-Cyber-Science-Technology.

[178] Paul McLeary, 'US Army Plans to Cut 3 of 13 Aviation Brigades by 2019', *Defense News*, 4 March 2014, http://www.defensenews.com/article/20140304/DEFREG02/303040040/US-Army-Plans-Cut-3-13-Aviation-Brigades-by-2019.

[179] Eli Lake, 'Obama Stresses Nation Building at Home Over Nation Building Abroad', *The Daily Beast*, 24 January 2014, www.thedailybeast.com/articles/2012/01/24/obama-stresses-nation-building-at-home-over-nation-building-abroad.html.

[180] Ronald Brownstein, 'Why Isolationism Is Back in America', *Defense One*, 6 September 2013, www.defenseone.com/politics/2013/09/why-isolationism-back-america/70026/.

[181] Pew Research, Center for the People and the Press, 17 January 2013, www.people-press.org/2013/01/17/section-1-obama-job-rating-personal-traits-views-of-michelle-obama/.

[182] Bruce Stokes, 'Public Opinion May Restrict Obama's Second-Term Foreign Policy', Chatham House 17 December 2013, http://www.chathamhouse.org/media/comment/view/196320.

[183] Brownstein, 'Why Isolationism Is Back in America'.

Arab uprisings

Despite the clearly articulated intention of the Obama administration to refocus away from the Middle East towards Asia, the continuing fallout of the 2011 Arab uprisings has made this difficult and looks likely to continue to do so in the foreseeable future.

Combined with its fiscal constraints and inwardly focused political climate, it is clear that the United States will have to make tough decisions about where to commit finite (and perhaps increasingly limited) resources. It is highly likely that these decisions may often mean trying to balance between solving immediate crises in the Middle East and attempting to maintain a longer-term shift towards Asia. The two principal figures behind the focus on Asia in President Obama's first term – Secretary of State Clinton and Assistant Secretary of State for East Asia and the Pacific Kurt Campbell – have left government. While the administration continues to support the rebalance, and Secretary of State Kerry and Secretary of Defense Hagel have made numerous trips to the region, Kerry has a long-standing personal involvement and interest in the Middle East. To the extent that his time is constrained, this appears to be where his attention is focused. Not having the same senior-level focus on the Asia-Pacific region means that the current leadership has less will to move tough agendas forward.

The withdrawal of US troops from Iraq in 2011 and from Afghanistan later in 2014 gives the United States more flexibility. However, as the instability in Iraq, the uncertainty in Egypt and civil war in Syria continue, it is unlikely that it will be able to turn its attention away from this region. The Middle East has bedevilled US policy-makers for decades and the optimism during the early days of the Arab uprisings that this could change has all but evaporated.

Changing US leverage and influence

While the trends above are affecting America's interests, capabilities and will to act, they are also affecting the perceptions of others in the Asia-Pacific region regarding the United States and its engagement. This has implications for America's leverage and influence.

As mentioned earlier, while the intention of the United States in announcing the rebalancing was to bring clarity to its continued engagement in the region, this was not the result that ensued. Instead there has been significant confusion over whether the initiative was new or not (President George H.W. Bush started the strategic rebalancing in the late 1980s) and what new assets or capabilities it might involve. It also suggested to some that this might be a temporary change, raising questions about America's long-term reliability.

Much of this uncertainty still remains despite ongoing efforts by the Obama administration to once again clarify its intentions. Doubts exist over America's reliability among some of its most important allies such as Japan and South Korea. This is beginning to affect the choices that these allies make to ensure their security over the long term.

This has begun to have an effect on the impact of America's actions in the region. Other trends such as China's economic rise have also changed the perceptions of US power. Today, the uncertainty and the perception of a weaker America with perhaps less will to act have changed the degree to which America's allies and others will depend on it and have affected their analysis of the circumstances under which it will act. This makes it even harder for the United States to calibrate its actions with those of its regional allies.

Regional perspectives on the US role

As stated in the 2012 Chatham House report *Prepared for Future Threats? US Defence Partnerships in the Asia-Pacific Region*, the US military presence in the region has four principal objectives: reassurance, dissuasion, deterrence and defeating any attacks. While there may be differences regarding how its partners believe the United States can best meet these objectives, they do want to see a continued US presence to ensure they are achieved. However, the differing interests among America's friends lead to a lack of consensus across the region about what they want from it and what kind of a role they would like it to take in the future. This makes developing an appropriately balanced US presence difficult.

Australia

Given its isolation in the south, Australia recognizes that alone it will never have the capabilities to protect all its surrounding maritime territory and that it needs the United States to maintain sufficient assets regionally – from surveillance capabilities to carrier groups – to assist in this. Australia has therefore accepted that it must offer the United States reciprocal support.

Japan

As Japan comes out of the economic doldrums and finds new political leadership, it is adopting a more assertive security stance with regard to its unilateral capabilities, expanding its defence assets and taking a more open interpretation of its constitution. This is, in part, to ensure it is less dependent on an uncertain America. In the meantime, however, while it still feels itself susceptible to Chinese pressure, it wants to ensure US deterrence, meaning a continued US presence. As Japanese capabilities develop, and given the political cost of maintaining US assets on Okinawa in particular, this could slowly change. Nevertheless, Japan is unlikely ever to look for US disengagement from the region.

South Korea

South Korea has great sensitivities with regard to China given the role that the latter will play in any eventual resolution of the all-important North Korean question. Thus while it depends fundamentally on US military capabilities for its security, it is also wary of antagonizing China or being seen as too close to the United States (and thus not to be trusted as an eventual post-reunification neighbour). Particularly while it continues to have concerns over its own capabilities, South Korea is therefore trying to maintain a careful balance between retaining the current military structure and relationship with the United States (or even enhancing it) and not causing a negative reaction by China. The status quo is its preferred option.

India

India is very sensitive to any perception that it might be dependent on, or be anything less than an equal to, the United States. It is careful to maintain its independence, even while it conducts a bilateral strategic dialogue. For this reason, while there have been a number of bilateral military agreements between them, it is extremely unlikely that there would ever be a formal alliance (at least in the coming decade). It does not perceive the same need as many of the other regional actors for a strong US regional presence to enhance its security, and as such any changes in US regional activity are likely to raise tensions or questions rather than to be embraced. On the other hand, India does have a similar goal to the United States with regard to ensuring that smaller countries in the region have foreign policy choices and can resist pressure from China or other big actors.

Singapore

Singapore maintains a strong relationship with the United States but one that is lacking in formal treaty-based ties, thus providing it with plenty of flexibility to manage its relationships both with that country and with China. It is unlikely to argue for a deeper military US presence in the region but welcomes and encourages the benefits of a strong relationship, including in the form of new US littoral ships. It too would not like to see less engagement by America.

Indonesia

Indonesia prefers to hold off developing formal relationships with either the United States or China, so maintaining its independence from both. With regard to the United States, therefore, while Indonesia has a strong working relationship, it is not inclined to support a stronger US presence, military or otherwise, that could upset the balance.

Others

A number of the other Southeast Asian countries, given their nervousness about China (particularly in the cases of the Philippines and Vietnam, with which it has territorial disputes) are very desirous of a continued, strong and relatively assertive role for the United States in the region. However, their dependence on China economically leads many to prefer an American presence that does not antagonize it and focuses on non-military aspects as well as the military relationship.

While all the parties concerned have strong and in many cases long-standing relationships with the United States, they are all looking for slightly different things from it. While all can probably agree on the need for a more engaged and assertive America in the diplomatic and, particularly, economic spheres, this is not necessarily also true in the military arena. In the area of security, the status quo is the preferred option for some, while others look for a more active US role. There is no consensus across the region.

If one moves out of the military arena and into diplomacy and economics, there is far more comfort and flexibility over America's regional engagement. Such emphasis is believed to be of far less concern to China and less likely to lead to potential conflict or rising tensions. It also provides the opportunity for the United States to be a counterweight to China's rising economic leverage, so fulfilling the desire of many of these countries to diversify their economic relations.

At the same time as the views of policy-makers both in and out of government are changing, so too are views of the United States on the part of the general public in the Asia-Pacific region. Polling has shown that the global image of both America and the American people have been in flux in the past decade, having recovered from the impact of US-led invasion of Iraq in 2003. In many countries the US ratings improved with the election of Barack Obama, but by 2013 approval for the United States had more or less returned to 2002 levels in most countries around the world. In the Asia-Pacific region, the attitudes of various countries towards America generally follow this pattern. For instance, Japan, while remaining an important pro-American power in the region, has seen a drop in favourability towards the United States from 72% in 2002 to 50% in 2008. This has since risen back to 69% in 2013. Australia recorded a drop of a similar magnitude, from 59% in 2003 to 46% in 2008, rising back to 66% in 2013. More dramatic still, 61% of Indonesians viewed America positively in 2002, but a year later the figure had dropped to 15%. It has since recovered to 61% in 2013.[184]

Asia-Pacific Security: A Changing Role for the United States
Responses

---

[184] Pew Research, Global Attitudes Project, 18 July 2013, www.pewglobal.org/2013/07/18/chapter-1-attitudes-toward-the-united-states/.

5. Looking Ahead

In an area as dynamic as the Asia-Pacific region, the future is particularly uncertain. This chapter does not attempt to be a comprehensive assessment of all the changes that could take place there, but instead provides an analysis of the major trends that can be anticipated, how they are likely to interact and, therefore, what kind of security capabilities are required, what kind of partnerships should be built, how regional organizations might be used, and what kind of a role might be appropriate for the United States.

A long-term perspective is necessary as it can take a decade (or more) for governments to change policy, for industry to ramp up production and for research and development to realize the solutions to growing challenges. Thus, while protection against today's security threats is needed, at the same time tomorrow's threats must be planned for, and the processes to achieve those goals started. Such a longer-term vision is the only insurance against the obstacles a country will face and reassurance of its ability to withstand an attack on its security.

The actors

There is great volatility in the Asia-Pacific region caused by new leaders, changing demographics, environmental concerns, democratic developments, and rising and falling powers. China, India and Indonesia (and to a lesser degree Vietnam) are on the rise; Japan's overt security role is in flux; Burma's future path is still highly unpredictable; Thailand's democracy is unstable; and North Korea's trajectory highly uncertain. However, a number of trends are likely to be witnessed.

Economic growth

While there is a chance that China will implode in the coming decades (those who take this view cite its overleveraged economy and excess capacity in many industries as major hidden risks), this scenario is less likely than the alternative – that its economy will continue to grow and, in so doing, add to its regional leverage.[185] China's relatively high economic growth rate, large population and ability thus far to withstand internal pressures, in combination with the leadership's recent apparent attention to reform (although this could be merely for show or a purging of specific individuals), raises confidence that it will remain able to pursue its current path and maintain stability. On the other hand, its GDP growth is likely to continue to slow, perhaps falling below the estimated rate (around 7.5%) at which the Communist Party is able to ensure the population's standard of living is maintained.

The economies of Japan (the third largest in the world) and India (the 10th largest) are expected to continue to rise (although there are uncertainties given 'Abe-nomics' in Japan and the corruption challenges in India). Other established economies in the region include Australia, South Korea and Indonesia, ranked 12th, 15th and 16th in the world respectively.[186] Malaysia and Vietnam enjoy a growth rate of 5.6% and 5.2% respectively, giving them the potential to become bigger economic players in the region.[187] In view of the concerns of many countries in the region regarding their respective economic dependence on China, it is likely that their reciprocal trade and investment will strengthen (particularly given the ASEAN free trade area). If the TPP is completed in the coming years, trade among many of these countries (excluding China and South Korea) will rise further.

While the region is susceptible to contagion, particularly if China's economic path becomes more unstable, given its many centres of growth (including India, Indonesia, Japan and the United States) it is likely that the region as a whole will continue to grow in the coming decade. The increasing diversity of rising economic powers provides stability and alternatives if some falter. While the burgeoning economic integration through such initiatives as the ASEAN free trade area makes them all more dependent on one another, it also creates a more level playing field for accessing markets, thus enhancing growth prospects. If the TPP is completed, this will further strengthen such outreach and engagement. This economic integration will also support security integration and diversify risk.

Democratic uncertainty

Several states in Asia are going through potentially major transitions towards or away from the status of stable democracies. These transformations and the associated instability will play a significant role in the ability of these countries and their neighbours to focus and work together on foreign policy rather than react to domestic upheavals. The overall trend here is not necessarily towards or away from democracy, but instead towards greater uncertainty in the coming decade.

China's political transition is very much in question: whether it can continue to open up economically while remaining closed politically has been long debated and

---

[185] Minxin Pei, 'China on verge of worst economic crisis in decades', CNN, 4 September 2013, http://globalpublicsquare.blogs.cnn.com/2013/09/04/china-on-verge-of-worst-economic-crisis-in-decades/.

[186] World Bank, 'Data: GDP Rankings, 2011–2012', as of February 2014, http://data.worldbank.org/data-catalog/GDP-ranking-table.

[187] CIA, World Factbook, 2012 estimates as of February 2014, www.cia.gov/library/publications/the-world-factbook/rankorder/2003rank.html.

plays out in the streets and on social media. Finding the balance is manifestly high among President Xi's priorities. And, while no one questions the longevity of India's democracy, over the past 18 months the rise of an anti-corruption drive and the appearance and success in the Delhi elections of the anti-corruption Aam Aadmi Party has led some to question whether the upcoming national elections will lead to a shake-up of the long-standing political coalition politics dominated by the main national parties, the Bharatiya Janata Party and Congress.

Since 2011, Burma has been in the midst of a significant political change away from a militarily run authoritarian government to a more democratic system. Its future is still very much in the balance and will depend, in part, on international diplomatic and economic support, as well as foreign direct investment. The political situation in Thailand has been unstable for at least the last five years. While the previous alternations of power have largely played out through a democratic electoral process, this is no longer the case: the opposition has called for the current government led by Prime Minister Yingluck Shinawatra to resign and for an unelected People's Council to undertake reforms. Other countries in the region, including Indonesia, Cambodia, Malaysia, and potentially even Singapore, also are showing some signs of transition.

Military expansion

With the exception of Japan until recently, military spending in in the region has been trending upwards (in particular since 2000) and, given the potential security challenges, there is little reason to believe that this will stop.[188] Potentially, the most significant shift in the last few years is in Japan, where Prime Minister Abe is pushing forward a reinterpretation of the constitutional limit on self-defence. He has also raised defence spending to 1% of GDP in 2013 and further increases have been intimated. Overall, military spending in Asia will continue to expand faster than in Europe and the United States. In 2011, for the first time, Asia (including Australasia) outspent Europe.[189] This must be seen in the context of the spending disparity between the United States and all other countries. However, the United States will continue to be by far the highest military spender and thus retain enormous advantages in this area. Meanwhile, while China has seen the largest growth in military expenditure, it must be remembered that over 50% of this is spent on internal security.[190]

It is also necessary to look at the countries' capabilities and where the spending is being applied. In terms of capabilities, the actions, joint operations (and training) that the United States and a number of regional friends and allies have undertaken over the past decade ensure that the level of readiness of these countries is higher and collaboration among them is likely to be more effective. At the same time, technological capabilities are, at least for the moment, rising faster in the United States (also, in part, driven by high operational levels) than elsewhere.

Overall, military spending in Asia will continue to expand faster than in Europe and the United States. In 2011, for the first time, Asia outspent Europe.

With regard to spending, China is focusing on increasing its power projection but does so from a relatively low base. However, there is little question that in the maritime space, its relative capabilities are rising along with its ability to take anti-access/area denial actions. India and others are reacting to this by expanding their naval capabilities. A number of the major powers are also beginning to focus on the more non-traditional areas of space and cyber security (both offensive and defensive). New cyber initiatives are being developed in, at least, China, India and Japan, although it is hard to analyse their relative capabilities given the lack of public information. China's developments in space, however, are probably the biggest game-changer in the past five years. As for Japan, it is still unclear how the reinterpretation of its constitution will alter the military balance of power. But the likely scenario – whereby Japan could now come to the assistance of allies in a conflict – could fundamentally rebalance the military equation in their favour.

Soft power stasis

There is little reason to believe that there will be significant changes with regard to the soft-power balance in the region. Asian universities, particularly those in China and Japan, are increasingly achieving high global rankings. Six universities based in Japan, Hong Kong, Singapore and South Korea, as well as two based in China, made it into the top 50 universities in the world rankings of 2013–14.[191] China's soft power, on the rise at the beginning of the 21st century, has diminished somewhat as a consequence of its

[188] 'China leads rise in Asia military spending', Agence France-Presse, 15 October 2012, http://www.rappler.com/world/14252-china-leads-rise-in-asia-military-spending.

[189] IISS, *The Military Balance 2014*, pp. 31, 488.

[190] Calum MacLeod, 'China boosts military and domestic security spending', *USA Today*, 5 March 2013, www.usatoday.com/story/news/world/2013/03/05/china-party-congress-military/1964405/.

[191] *Times Higher Education*, 'World University Rankings 2013–2014', as of February 2014, www.timeshighereducation.co.uk/world-university-rankings/2013-14/world-ranking/region/asia.

military muscle-flexing. Japan's soft power also is limited by the long memories of its neighbours regarding Japanese aggression in the Second World War. These memories are slow to fade and Abe's recent military and diplomatic initiatives have not helped. His visit to the Yasukuni shrine in December 2013 was seen in the region as particularly offensive. Indonesia has seen an increase in its soft power that could well continue, depending, in part, on the outcome of the July 2014 elections. India's relatively recent loss of soft power, stemming from its political, demographic and corruption challenges in particular, is likely to restabilize in the coming years.

Regional relationships

The balance of power in the Asia-Pacific region should be seen in the context of all the principal players – at a minimum, the United States, China, India, Japan and perhaps Indonesia – rather than the often posited, more limited US–Chinese bipolarity. As China's GDP growth continues to slow and the United States regains its economic footing, as India and Japan both find new paths to growth, and as Indonesia continues its democratic path, great-power relations in the region will be more diversified than they are often perceived today.

This growth in the number of major actors in the region will be accompanied by a concomitant thickening of bilateral and plurilateral relationships between them and others in the region, as well as the likely (slow but steady) strengthening of some regional groups, such as ASEAN. These trends are likely to lead to more diversification and greater integration of the principal players, and to a more balanced geopolitical framework that is far more nuanced and flexible than the current simplistic bipolar model.

Despite the widespread desire, particularly in the United States and Japan, for Japan and South Korea to work more closely together on regional challenges, it is unlikely that any significant progress in this respect will be made, unless it is driven by an outside threat (such as a significantly more aggressive China or a major regional cyber attack). In the absence of such an external impetus, the historical antagonisms between the two countries will continue to prevent closer relations. Nevertheless, it is conceivable that small steps in specific areas could be taken, such as the joint agreement to cooperate in intelligence-sharing, if a threat were perceived and the circumstances were right.

Given Prime Minister Abe's nationalistic stance, in particular with regard to reinforcing and extending Japan's self-defence capabilities as well as his visit to Yasukuni shrine, he is likely to find it hard to improve relations with many countries in the region, in particular those that suffered under Japanese occupation during the Second World War.

Others such as Australia and India, however, might in fact find the new, more robust Japan of greater interest and potential in terms of military-to-military partnerships, particularly as it becomes more able to act overseas in support of allies.

India too is in a state of some flux. Despite its current political and economic challenges, it is likely to continue to expand its military, particularly its naval forces, and to patrol more actively and heighten diplomatic engagement with countries in the Asia-Pacific region. If the opposition BJP wins the coming elections, its stronger 'Hindutva' nationalism could lead to a more assertive India and one that prioritizes military and strategic strength. Many in the region, especially the smaller ASEAN states, might support a more assertive India as an 'outside' power that can provide some balance to China. India's growing informal engagements with other powers in the region, including Japan, Australia and Indonesia, will continue. Its desire to protect the sea lanes on which it depends for energy and trade, to enhance its regional and global role and reputation, and to break out of what some perceive as a Chinese containment strategy (the 'string of pearls'), will support this expansion strategy.

Finally, while there are some concerns regarding the Indonesian elections in July 2014, it is expected that the country will continue to pursue a position of leadership in Southeast Asia and especially in ASEAN. While Indonesia currently pursues its foreign policy through ASEAN, and will maintain its efforts to develop the organization's role and influence, it is likely to start to take a stronger unilateral approach as well. Indonesia has already pursued such a strategy in some cases, not least towards India and Australia.

America's future capabilities

The Obama administration has made clear its intention for the United States to remain an Asian power, and this is a bipartisan strategic objective. However, while the United States intends to increase its military (and other) engagement with the region, given capability increases, resource constraints and changes in domestic attitudes to intervention, it is likely to recalibrate its needs in this area, leading to an eventual decrease in military personnel numbers. Asia will have to accept, as Europe does today, that the United States no longer has either the will or the capacity to extend itself in ways that are not of direct vital national interest. This trend is likely to be compounded by the growth of Asia, both economically and militarily. Put simply, as Asia becomes stronger the relatively shrinking United States will no longer be quite as powerful an actor in the region.

This is not an indication of US withdrawal or isolationism, however. Even if US defence spending continues to decline, it will for a long while remain vastly larger than that the total defence expenditure of the Asian powers and many times larger than Chinese spending.[192] A less engaged America in the Asia-Pacific region is not an inactive or absent one. It will still have interests in the region, not the least of which will be supporting its allies and friends and maintaining stability. But a more equitable burden-sharing is likely to develop.

At the same time as there are defence cuts, the remaining US assets need to be able to act against an increasing array of traditional and non-traditional threats. Thus it is not just the numbers that will change, but also the makeup of American forces and how they are balanced. A different type of capability and presence is required. Changes in response to these differing threats are already taking place. Cuts in the US army, and to a lesser extent the navy and air force, are being compensated by an increase in cyber-capabilities. Intelligence, surveillance and reconnaissance (ISR) capabilities are also being expanded by increased investment in programmes such as the Predator, Global Hawk and Shadow unmanned aerial vehicles. Such technologies are proving vital to US forces in all services and allow them to have greater impact and reach. Allies in the region will need to adjust to these changing capabilities. In some countries (in particular Singapore, Japan and Australia), this is already beginning to affect the allocation of resources and broader defence planning.

The challenges

As the regional powers in this study look to the future, beyond the challenges due to natural resource constraints, the perceived likely instigators of threats remain largely the same: China, North Korea, terrorists and insurgent groups. Man-made threats are likely to be imposed less through traditional military actions and more through non-traditional means including cyber-attacks, attacks on communications satellites, and economic and natural-resource constraints.

China

It is hoped that the Chinese–US relationship will become more stable and perhaps strengthen over the coming 15 years. However, given China's power and its uncertain path, it will remain the focus of attention among others in the region. Conflict is most likely to break out through unintentional escalation, in which China or some other actor inadvertently crosses a red line and sets off a sequence of events. If China, Japan and others continue to expand their military capabilities, this scenario will become more likely, particularly given China's efforts to expand its power projection capabilities, providing it with a longer reach and therefore more chance of coming into contact with the militaries of other countries.

While such a scenario could occur today, what is likely to change in the coming years is how China (or others) act in response to the potential conflict. New trends are already being seen. The following escalatory steps (from which it could be easier to back down) are likely to be pursued on the way to full-blown conflict for which countries need to be prepared:

1. *Cyber-warfare:* Cyber-war can be waged without troops crossing borders or significant numbers of soldiers (or civilians) being killed. It can be implemented without a declaration of war. It is already being waged in some areas as governments build in weaknesses or back doors in adversaries' systems, so allowing them future pressure points or access. The revelations made by the former US intelligence contractor Edward Snowden suggest that the United States may already be doing this. Further evidence indicates that others, such as China, are also pursuing such a strategy.

2. *Economic and natural-resource warfare:* Economic warfare can be conducted simultaneously with cyber-warfare. Examples of economic warfare are already evident and could escalate to situations where countries cut off financial flows, prevent international organizations from providing funding, stop the export or import of necessary goods and resources (whether minerals, energy, food or water), and formally impose sanctions.

3. *Conflict in outer space:* As tensions ratchet up and it becomes more likely that traditional warfare might take place, attacks in the space arena, to bring down or disrupt military and communications satellites, would also occur. Despite efforts in multilateral forums to create an international agreement to prevent warfare in space, progress has been very slow.

4. *Air and maritime war:* If events continue to escalate, more traditional instruments will be used between the adversaries as trade flows are disrupted, area denial is attempted and territorial waters are entered.

---

[192] US spending is currently around 3.7% of GDP and in 2013 totalled $600bn including on Afghanistan, compared with the estimate for China of $112bn in the same period. US spending accounts for 39% of total global defence expenditures. IISS, *The Military Balance 2014*.

5. *Ground war:* It is extremely unlikely that a full-scale ground war will take place between China and any of the countries on which this study focuses, even if smaller-scale conflicts over territory could break out. There is some risk, however, that such smaller conflicts could escalate.

North Korea

The most likely major change in the next 15 years or so will come from North Korea. While the North Korean elite is doing everything in its power to retain control (with a total lack of concern for the public), as it has done quite successfully for decades, this strategy will become harder to sustain, given the growing economic and environmental challenges and the difficulty of keeping people uninformed. The two scenarios below are possible over the coming years.

Regime collapse
The regime will collapse (quite possibly quickly and without warning) either through a coup or revolution (perhaps supported from outside). There would then be two alternative paths for events, depending predominantly on China's actions. Either a new leader will be appointed *de facto* by China, or North and South Korea will be reunited. In both cases, one of the greatest concerns will be ensuring the protection of North Korea's nuclear capabilities. However, with new leadership in place, it is likely that the nation will be able to rejoin the international community.

A weaker status quo
North Korea under Kim Jong-Un will retain its independence, but its power will steadily diminish (and perhaps as a result it will become more volatile) as the challenge of feeding and meeting the needs of its people becomes greater. As the social situation worsens, North Korea will become more dangerous as it looks for an outside enemy to blame. The increasing access to external information by North Koreans will make it harder for the current regime to remain in power without increasingly harsh measures, thus further stoking internal tensions and instability.

As North Korea feels threatened it will once again hit out against its neighbours, in particular South Korea. But as with China, it is increasingly likely to do so (as it already has) through unconventional means such as cyber-attacks. Given its economic challenges, it will find low-risk (i.e. more deniable) and low-cost attacks particularly attractive.

Terrorism and insurgency

The level of terrorism has decreased over the past decade in the Asia-Pacific region. While the increase in extremism in the Middle East and elsewhere might have repercussions and flow into the region, at present, and in the medium term, it appears likely to remain a steady-state concern but not rise above this.

Domestic insurgency will continue to be of concern in some states. Despite progress over the past decade in reaching peace agreements with a number of organizations in Indonesia and the Philippines, many disagreements remain and, as seen recently in Malaysia, groups that have felt left out of a negotiating process still have the capabilities to cause great violence.[193] Unless governments can find mutually agreeable solutions with insurgents, such threats will remain. And, as events in Afghanistan and Syria have shown, if conflicts in the region were to regain their potency, fighters from Asia who have gone to other areas (such as Afghanistan, Iraq and Syria) could come flooding back with new skills and networks to support them.

> While the increase in extremism in the Middle East and elsewhere might have repercussions and flow into the region, at present, and in the medium term, it appears likely to remain a steady-state concern but not rise above this.

Once again, however, what is changing is how these actors are trying to achieve their ends. As the attacks in the Philippines by the Abu Sayyaf group and the Bangsamoro Islamic Freedom Fighters in 2013 showed, traditional kinetic attacks are still the most common form of action. However, the diffusion of new technologies, particularly in the areas of cyber and communications, mean that these groups or individuals will have new powerful instruments to use against their governments and the population, which are likely to proliferate.

Natural resources

As discussed in Chapter 3, the supply of natural resources is a growing area of concern for a number of countries across Asia. The consumption of resources, ranging from food to natural minerals, is increasing rapidly. Given the anticipated increases in populations and economic development, both of which drive consumption, these constraints will only get tighter in the coming decades, leading to greater competition.

---

[193] In March 2013, a Muslim clan from the Philippines invaded Malaysia asserting a long-held claim to Sabah.

Much of this competition is taking place outside the region, in currently less developed regions such as Africa. China and more recently India have been heavy investors in natural resources in Africa in order to tie them up. However, in some cases the suppliers are closer to home. Water, oil and gas are all prevalent in the Asia-Pacific and surrounding areas and have been the driver of rising tensions and conflict. As the constraints become more painful, these tensions could well rise further and spiral out of control. This is particularly the case for some of the islands where oil and gas resources are tied to the territorial disputes.

Although Indonesia is particularly aware of the potential food and water threats to its people, there will be implications for all the countries concerned.

What domestic capability changes will there be?

There has been a dramatic increase in defence expenditure over the past decade in Asia. China and India make up a significant proportion of this spending, but Indonesia, Japan and Singapore have also seen rises.[194] Since GDP has also increased in most of these countries, however, the proportions being spent on defence remains relatively static (except for India, South Korea and Singapore, where it is falling).

Figure 6: Asian defence spending as a proportion of GDP (selected countries)

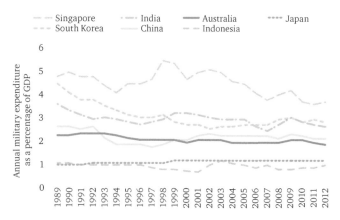

Source: SIPRI Military Expenditure Database.[195]

Despite these spending increases, it is unlikely that straight-line projections made today will be confirmed over the coming 15 or so years. GDP growth in both India and China is slowing, with likely implications for their defence spending. In most countries in the region, the spending increase has translated into more advanced military equipment. For example, increased budgets (approximately $2 billion between 2012 and 2013) have allowed India to purchase new naval vessels and heavy-lift helicopters.

Japan's expenditure increase to 1% of GDP will allow it to acquire significantly more equipment and/or undertake more training, but this too is likely to plateau. In the coming years it is likely to take a much broader interpretation of the role of its Self Defense Force, including increasing activities beyond its borders, to supporting allies (in particular the United States) when they are attacked, and building the ability to strike first at an adversary's missile-launch facilities.[196] Japan has also put resources into improving its cyber defence as well as its national security structures with the establishment of a National Security Council and the publication of its National Security Strategy for the first time in December 2013.

The repercussions of this increase and then plateauing of defence spending in Asia is that domestic security capabilities will improve for most of the countries concerned in the next 15 years. Like European countries, the Asia-Pacific states have no history of 'pooling and sharing' security resources and the primacy of sovereignty still far exceeds the perceived need to collaborate in this area. Given the rise in defence capabilities in the big powers, their relative positions are unlikely to change significantly, except in specific arenas such as naval off-shoring capabilities (the ability to extend naval forces beyond one's borders), drones, intelligence and surveillance assets, and cyber capabilities, where focus on one or the other could change the balance in the margins.

One of the goals of the Indian and Japanese militaries, in particular in the light of perceived ongoing encroachment by China, is to focus on power projection. Japan has recently beefed up its coastguard – the closest it can come to such expansion under the current interpretation of the constitution.[197] India is focusing on expanding its naval assets not just in the Indian Ocean but also in the South China Sea.[198] But these expanded capabilities will lead to an increasing risk of friction with China, which is also acting similarly with its AA/AD strategy. This could lead to more

---

[194] IISS, *The Military Balance 2013*, pp. 245–352.

[195] See http://www.sipri.org/research/armaments/milex/milex_database/milex_database.

[196] 'Surrounded by sharks', *The Economist*, 18 January 2014, www.economist.com/news/asia/21594351-japans-relationship-united-states-attendant-rise-china-surrounded-sharks.

[197] Tiago Mauricio, 'PacNet #60 – Abenomics and Japan's Defense Priorities', Centre for Strategic and International Studies, 5 August 2013, https://csis.org/files/publication/Pac1360.pdf.

[198] Chietigj Bajpaee, 'Reaffirming India's South China Sea Credentials', *The Diplomat*, 14 August 2013, http://thediplomat.com/2013/08/reaffirming-indias-south-china-sea-credentials/.

incidents like the near-clash in December 2013 between US and Chinese vessels in the South China Sea.

This trend towards greater power-projection capabilities is also probably a response to the perception that America's role in providing regional (particularly maritime) security will diminish. Despite the rebalance, some of America's allies, in particular, have expanded their off-shore capabilities to ensure that sea lanes remain open given greater uncertainty over active US engagement.

Indonesia also is likely to continue to increase its defence spending. As its security concerns are principally domestic, it will maintain military capabilities that are able to respond to insurgent threats. However, as the battle over natural resources becomes fiercer and the military capabilities of other countries improve, Indonesia too will try to maintain its leverage in these areas. The long hiatus in US–Indonesian military engagement, following the imposition of the Leahy Amendment, means that Indonesia is starting from a relatively low base with regard to training and equipment, at least as far as the United States is concerned. There is much space for improved engagement.

Given the challenges India faces domestically, politically, economically and with regard to corruption, it is unlikely that its significantly increased military spending will continue unabated over the coming two decades. While, according to Prime Minister Singh, the greatest perceived threat is that of insurgent groups, the military is focused very much at the external threat, where the pendulum continues to swing between Pakistan and China. India is also building domestic capabilities in cyber defence. In January it announced it would soon set up a Tri-Service Cyber Command to deal with the growth in cyber-attacks.[199]

The most profound change within South Korea over the coming years will be the transfer of leadership and responsibility over the military from US to South Korean control in the event of a conflict. This transfer has been delayed repeatedly and has a current deadline of 2015. In the meantime, the United States announced in January 2014 that it was going to add an additional 800 troops (plus equipment) to the 28,500 already in South Korea, probably in response to uncertainty over North Korea.[200]

Neither Singapore nor Australia, barring any new unpredictable event, is likely to see a significant increase in defence capabilities in the coming decade. Maintenance of current capabilities is likely to be the priority, although there are efforts in Australia to upgrade certain areas, as seen, for example, in the planned purchase of 72 F-35 Joint Strike Fighters.[201] Australia has recently oscillated in its view of the threat from China. The current government is more nationalistic than its predecessor and wants to focus more on regional issues. It has pledged to increase defence spending to 2% of GDP.

It is worth also noting that most of the defence spending detailed above reflects traditional military capabilities – armies, navies, air forces etc. However, given that the threats are likely to move into unconventional areas such as space, food and water, energy or cyber security, only some of which can be partially countered by the military, it is rarely likely to be the most effective tool.

In the cyber realm, however, some of the countries in question are focusing on upgrading their resources. India, Japan and South Korea in particular have invested increased resources and created cyber commands of various types, and instituted new processes or systems to explore these threats. However, there appears to be little real cooperation between these countries (or with the United States) in this area despite the inherent transnational nature of the threats. What cooperation there is (such as between the United States and India) occurs in the margins.

Unlike defence spending, expenditure on other instruments of power such as diplomacy or on agricultural technologies (to improve food and water security) is unlikely to see the same focus. Relatively speaking, most countries, notably India, have remarkably small diplomatic capabilities for their size and GDP.[202] Given the increasing emergence of non-traditional threats, additional resources – financial, personnel and particularly political – need to be urgently focused in these areas. This is not yet taking place in any meaningful way.

How will domestic capabilities be supported by regional or plurilateral alliances?

Given the disparities of interests and intentions within the membership of the major Asia-Pacific countries it is unlikely that regional groups will be able to develop into stronger, more active institutions (similar to NATO or the European Union). Arguably the most important body, ASEAN, will not

[199] Pradip R. Sagar, 'India readies cyber command service to combat espionage threats online', DNA India, 15 January 2014, www.dnaindia.com/india/report-india-readies-cyber-command-service-to-combat-espionage-threats-online-1950997.

[200] Tony Capaccio and Nicole Gaouette, 'US adding 800 troops for South Korea citing rebalance', Bloomberg News, 7 January 2014, www.bloomberg.com/news/2014-01-07/u-s-adding-800-troops-for-south-korea-citing-rebalance.html.

[201] Nigel Pittaway, 'Australia's F-35 Buy Unaffected by US Sequestration', Defense News, 31 October 2013, www.defensenews.com/article/20131031/DEFREG03/310310023/Australia-s-F-35-Buy-Unaffected-by-US-Sequestration.

[202] Sudha Ramachandra, 'The Indian Foreign Service: Worthy of an Emerging Power?', The Diplomat, 12 July 2013, http://thediplomat.com/2013/07/the-indian-foreign-service-worthy-of-an-emerging-power/.

take a more assertive role, held back by its members' lack of desire for a more powerful organization or their inability to agree upon specific actions. Some even suggest that the institution will become less relevant over time. If China continues to impose strong assertive pressure on its allies within ASEAN (as is currently the case with Cambodia), this may even split the organization.

The other significant security institution in the region, the EAS, is also unlikely to take a more active role. While the inclusion of all the major regional powers (including China, the United States, Russia, India, Australia, Japan and South Korea) makes it an important forum for discussion, it also ensures that major initiatives are unlikely. Other smaller groups such as the SCO, while still relevant, are limited by the fact that they comprise only a subset of the important players.

By providing a credible voice for the smaller actors and a point for them to come together, as well as creating a mechanism through which broader conflicts could be discussed and addressed, ASEAN could provide a very important 'sponge' to soak up possible tensions.

These multiple forums could provide other regional benefits, however, particularly if one takes a longer time horizon. ASEAN in particular, with strong leadership from Indonesia and support from other states such as Singapore, could provide another gravitational pole around which smaller powers could coalesce. This is particularly true in the economic space (given the ASEAN FTA). As the larger powers manage their respective bilateral relations, by providing a credible voice for the smaller actors and a point for them to come together, as well as creating a mechanism through which broader conflicts could be discussed and addressed, ASEAN could provide a very important 'sponge' to soak up possible tensions.

As noted, ASEAN and other such forums are also well placed to address some of the non-traditional security concerns that will become more potent in the coming decades. While it is typically too controversial for these institutions to have a role in traditional military or security dilemmas where the issues are often perceived as zero-sum, in arenas such as cyber, space, food and water security, the global nature of the threat and its impact on all parties could make these venues more productive. These issues are more susceptible to decisive action in regional organizations where solutions are needed for challenges that many actors face and where all can benefit. It might even be possible to deal with cyber issues in these organizations (although distrust will inevitably limit what can be shared).

While the established groups are unable to implement concrete policy changes or act together on security initiatives, there is more space for other ad hoc groups to take some leadership roles. While they will, inevitably, be limited by the lack of legitimacy determined by their small membership, they can also provide the base from which to launch other initiatives (which can, as appropriate, be taken up by the broader forums). This trend towards more engaged ad hoc coalitions is similar to that seen elsewhere around the world. And, like these other initiatives, they are likely in time to coalesce around specific objectives such as anti-piracy measures or counter-terrorism.

Thus although formal groups will continue to show little leadership in traditional security matters, plurilateral groups are increasingly likely to fill that gap. While these informal partnerships have traditionally focused on less concrete activities such as training and diplomatic engagement, their remit could in time develop in two ways. In some cases, countries that have invested in strong strategic relationships, through either bilateral or plurilateral groups, could build formal alliances to come to one another's defence (though this will be made difficult by the same challenges that such alliances face today, such as lack of trust, historical antagonisms and varying interests). More likely, the alliances might centre around thematic goals (e.g. non-proliferation, anti-piracy measures or counter-terrorism) on which the members will find collaborative ways to work.

How will America's role change to address remaining gaps?

As mentioned earlier, notwithstanding the rebalance to Asia, America's will and relative capabilities (if not its interests, which are more permanent) are likely to diminish over the coming 15 years. Thus its Asia-Pacific friends, allies and partners will have to respond to a new, less active, America in the region. This does not signify a reversal of the rebalance, but instead reflects America's changing role globally. It will shift from being the first 'go-to' country for regional (or national) stability and security, to an engaged partner, but not necessarily the leader. Already allies are responding to this new US role as they implicitly or explicitly explore new domestic capabilities or partnerships.

This disengagement is not all-encompassing. The United States will uphold its current security commitments, including, for example, to Taiwan, Japan and the Philippines. But at the same time, it will expect its allies to bear more of the burdens of leadership in the region. It will continue to reassure, dissuade, deter and defend, using its military, diplomatic, economic and other assets. If

America's interests are directly threatened, it will engage all its capabilities as needed to respond. Its ability to act should not be underestimated.

In the case of South Korea, the United States will shortly no longer be in the lead in a conflict. Despite the recent addition of 800 troops, over the coming decades it is likely that it will actually reduce the number of troops (and perhaps even bases) permanently stationed there. As has happened in Japan and Australia, it is likely that more use will be made of rotations. In Japan, domestic politics also point to an eventual US draw-down. A more accurate reflection of need and available resources is likely to drive this new agenda: new non-traditional threats are less susceptible to traditional military responses. At the same time, cuts in US defence spending are more likely to lead to the shutting down of overseas bases before those in the United States (despite the military position that the former are often more advantageous) owing to Congressional pressure as politicians strive to keep jobs at home.[203]

On the other hand, America's diplomatic and economic re-engagement in the region is likely to continue. While budgets continue to be tight at the State Department, leading figures in both parties as well as military and diplomatic officers have stated the importance of the civilian or diplomatic surge. Like many European countries, the United States will continue to rebalance its diplomatic and other resources to Asia. The growing emergence of new economic powers in the region, and their large populations, will also drive investment and trade (supported perhaps by the completion of the TPP).

Given the global nature of some of the rising threats – cyber, food, energy and water security – America will continue to be a necessary, if not sufficient, actor in addressing them. Thus its intellectual and entrepreneurial resources will remain focused on the region. These other instruments of US state power are generally less expensive to maintain than the military. And in many cases, they could be led not by the state but by non-state actors, from corporates to NGOs.

Where do the gaps remain?

As the 2012 Chatham House report on US defence partnerships in the Asia-Pacific region pointed out, the focus of the United States has been on addressing or mitigating traditional threats from adversaries. Even though, increasingly, threats are going to play out in non-traditional areas and thus require, at least in part, a non-military response, most states in the region, including those examined in this report (and the United States), continue to focus and add resources predominantly in the traditional arena.

However, many of these non-traditional threats, given their transborder nature, are best addressed regionally or plurilaterally rather than unilaterally. Increased investment in understanding and addressing the potential security challenges manifest through food, water, energy and other resource insecurity is vital. Member states will still need to develop their domestic understanding of these threats, and some strategic capabilities to address them (e.g. perhaps by diversifying their sourcing of energy or food), but possible solutions can also be achieved by sharing the challenge and finding common diplomatic or other solutions through regional organizations. Both these paths should be pursued.

Given the non-state nature of some of the threats and the greater power of individuals or groups to make an impact through cyber-terrorism or other forms of violence, these states will also need to find more effective ways of sharing information and intelligence. This will require trust.

---

[203] This is seen in Germany today where two out of four battalions are returning to the United States. Some US military officers have suggested that this is the wrong decision with regard to maintaining capabilities, partnership and interoperability, but is instead taking place owing to resource constraints and politics.

6. Conclusion

The United States' policy towards the Asia-Pacific region has emphasized both its own continued engagement and the desire to promote relations between its friends and allies. Like many in Europe, it sees great potential in building up regional organizations such as ASEAN (and its subsidiaries), the EAS and APEC, into more concrete forums for action. However, in all three cases, American and broader Western policy is going to find itself hampered by the differing interests of the Asia-Pacific partners themselves.

While America will stay engaged in the region in the coming decades, many of its allies and partners there have concerns about what they perceive to be America's increasing unreliability and lack of willingness to engage resources (diplomatic and potentially military) to defend their interests and meet their commitments. This has resulted in a quiet drive to enhance domestic capabilities to compensate. America will continue to be a partner in the region, but it is likely to be less the centre-point than has historically been the case.

America's efforts to promote closer relations between its allies, in particular Japan and South Korea, are also unlikely to make progress. The memories of Japan's actions in the Second World War are still too prominent in the minds of the South Korean elite and public, and Prime Minister Abe's efforts to reinterpret his country's constitution in the coming years will only heighten these concerns. Perhaps more profoundly, South Korea and Japanese interests, particularly with regard to China, are not aligned, making it unlikely that the two will work together in this area. These two factors – history and misaligned interests – play out to lesser degrees with many other countries.

Finally, the Western desire to see regional Asia-Pacific organizations, such as ASEAN and the EAS, develop into more concrete action-oriented institutions is contrary to the desire of their member states, which have no intention of giving up their sovereignty. There is no indication that these institutions will be anything more than they are today – principally talking shops. This role should not be underestimated, however, as it fulfils a very important regional function.

From an Asia-Pacific perspective, there are some significant changes taking place that will need to be addressed. First of all, while the six countries considered in this study have similar broad perceptions of threats, their prioritization of these differs, as do the details of their responses. This will make it hard for them to work closely together. However, as one looks to the future, they do have increasingly common interests in the growing non-traditional threats, from cyber security to economic, food and water security. Thus it is more likely that despite remaining differences in certain areas, common approaches and collaboration will be possible.

With the perception in some countries, most notably Japan and the Philippines, that the United States is no longer such a reliable ally, these countries and others are increasingly building their own domestic military capabilities to ensure their own security. But the United States remains an absolutely necessary partner. None of these countries see the formal regional organizations filling the gap, or replacing the role of the United States, although many are developing more regional bilateral and plurilateral relationships that could provide additional support in areas such as training and diplomatic engagement.

While America will stay engaged in the region in the coming decades, many of its allies and partners there have concerns about what they perceive to be America's increasing unreliability and lack of willingness to engage resources to defend their interests and meet their commitments.

Given the future threats developing in particular in the non-traditional areas, it is possible that the formal regional organizations and these bilateral and plurilateral groups (or ad hoc coalitions) could play a stronger role. While these organizations will not be militarily operational, many non-traditional challenges are best addressed through other instruments such as diplomacy and economic engagement, where they might be better placed to step in. This could, in time, result in a rise in their influence.

Meanwhile, groups such as ASEAN could also come to provide a useful 'sponge' function, soaking up wider tensions and potential conflicts between members and providing a more productive environment for discussion. This would be likely to diminish the otherwise bipolar perception of potential conflict that plays out between China and the United States by providing an alternative centre of gravity.

Finally, it is likely that, in this context, while the United States will continue to be an Asia-Pacific power and to provide a broad umbrella of security to the region, it will choose a less active role (in particular where military resources are required) except where its direct vital national interests are implicated. Allies will be expected to step up more instead. The United States will remain a necessary partner and actor in the region – *primus inter pares* – but it will also be only one of a number of such players.

Appendix: Major Regional Organizations

Association of Southeast Asian Nations (ASEAN)

Membership: Brunei, Burma (Myanmar), Cambodia, Indonesia, Laos, Malaysia, Philippines, Singapore, Thailand and Vietnam.

ASEAN was established in 1967 by Indonesia, Malaysia, the Philippines, Singapore, and Thailand. The organization was originally conceived to allow all member governments to focus on commonly perceived threats (particularly communism) and economic development, and also in part arose out of waning faith in external powers, with the aim of fostering economic and political dialogue among members. It was preceded by the Association of Southeast Asia (ASA), an alliance consisting of the Philippines, Malaysia and Thailand, formed in 1961.

Future trajectory: Despite making progress as an economic organization, ASEAN has not been as effective in mitigating territorial disputes between members. It is a consensus-driven organization that does not intervene in members' domestic affairs. Because of their differing views, members often pursue security issues bilaterally, and not within the multilateral forum.

The constituent countries of ASEAN have a strong potential for future economic growth that could be greatly enhanced if regional integration is successful. It is in this economic sphere that most agreement can be found among the ASEAN countries. However, in the security realm, there is far less consensus. There are a variety of territorial disputes both between member states and with other countries, particularly China, which could derail progress. While the majority of the member governments have made it clear that they do not want to see a more operational organization, Singapore and the informal leader, Indonesia, in particular, would be likely to lean towards an organization that had more teeth.

The United States participates in the organization's summits and has signed the ASEAN Treaty of Amity and Cooperation. It has established the annual US–ASEAN summit. In the economic sphere, while the US focus is on the TPP, for those Southeast Asian countries that are not participating in the TPP negotiations, the United States has launched the Expanded Economic Engagement (E3) initiative.

ASEAN-related organizations

ADMM and ADMM+

Membership: Defence ministers from ASEAN, plus those of the United States, China, Russia, Japan, India, South Korea, Australia and New Zealand.

The ASEAN Defence Ministers' Meeting (ADMM), established in 2006, is the highest defence mechanism within ASEAN. Its stated aim is to 'promote mutual trust and confidence through greater understanding of defence and security challenges as well as enhancement of transparency and openness'.[204] It has achieved this through hosting discussions on contemporary defence and security issues and the challenges facing the region.

The 2008–10 work programme identified five areas of focus: promoting regional defence and security cooperation, shaping and sharing of norms, conflict prevention, conflict resolution and post-conflict peace-building. In 2010, the ADMM+ was created to tackle five areas: maritime security, counter-terrorism, disaster management, peacekeeping operations and military medicine.[205]

This forum has strengthened cooperation between members in dealing with non-traditional security threats. They have also issued joint concept papers on the use of military capabilities in humanitarian assistance and disaster relief, cooperation on non-traditional security issues between the military and civil society, and linkages with non-ASEAN partners.

ADMM+ has also discussed terrorism, piracy, proliferation of weapons of mass destruction and some maritime issues such as the situation in the South China Sea. Given that this is the biggest source of discord between China and several ASEAN countries with overlapping territorial claims, the mere fact that it was discussed with the United States was an important step forward.

ASEAN Regional Forum (ARF)

Membership: Australia, Bangladesh, Brunei, Cambodia, Canada, China, European Union, India, Indonesia, Japan, North Korea, South Korea, Laos, Malaysia, Burma (Myanmar), Mongolia, New Zealand, Pakistan, Papua New Guinea, Philippines, Russia, Singapore, Sri Lanka, Thailand, Timor-Leste, United States, Vietnam.

---

[204] 'ASEAN Defence Ministers meet for security issue', Talk Vietnam, 1 May 2013, http://talkvietnam.com/2013/05/asean-defence-ministers-meet-for-security-issue/#.UvTysawcuW8.
[205] Association of Southeast Asian Nations, 'ASEAN Defence Ministers Meeting ADMM', www.asean.org/communities/asean-political-security-community/category/asean-defence-ministers-meeting-admm.

Launched in 1994, the objectives of the ARF are 'to foster constructive dialogue and consultation on political and security issues of common interest and concern; and to make significant contributions to efforts towards confidence-building and preventive diplomacy in the Asia-Pacific region'. As such the ARF is largely considered to be the 'security' arm of ASEAN. The ARF Experts and Eminent Persons Group (EEP), which met in 2013 in Hawaii, proposed 12 specific recommendations to the group including the development of ARF into a preventive diplomacy body.[206]

The ARF has a particularly sensitive portfolio focused on security, which has resulted in frequently (and increasingly) tense meetings – in particular, in 2012 over maritime tensions when China refused again to countenance discussions in multilateral forums of what it considers to be bilateral issues.[207]

ASEAN+1

Membership: ASEAN+ another nation (typically China but can be India, the United States and others).

The objective of these +1 groupings is to facilitate discussions and engagement between ASEAN and the other power. China has attended ASEAN conferences since 1991. Negotiations have focused quite extensively on economic issues (given China's resistance to engaging on security issues in a multilateral or plurilateral setting). Formal discussions with the United States and Japan started in 1977 (though informal discussions with Japan began in 1973).[208]

ASEAN+3

Membership: ASEAN+ Japan, China, South Korea.

ASEAN+3 manages cooperation between leaders, ministers and senior officials from ASEAN and the three major East Asia countries. The first leaders' meetings were held in 1996 and 1997 to deal with Asia–Europe issues, and afterwards both China and Japan wanted regular summit meetings with ASEAN members. The group's importance was strengthened by the Asian financial crisis of 1997, when ASEAN's response involved close cooperation with the three countries. Since the implementation of the Joint

Statement on East Asia Cooperation in 1999 at the Manila Summit, ASEAN+3 finance ministers have been holding periodic consultations. Once again, the tensest discussions typically revolve around maritime issues between the member states. Despite the rising political tensions at the 2012 and 2013 meetings, leaders agreed that there was a need to continue to strengthen financial cooperation and to work together to boost food security, among other issues.[209]

Asia-Pacific Economic Cooperation (APEC)

Membership: Australia, Brunei, Canada, Chile, China, Hong Kong, Indonesia, Japan, Malaysia, Mexico, New Zealand, Papua New Guinea, Peru, Philippines, Russia, Singapore, South Korea, Taiwan, Thailand, United States, Vietnam.

APEC's principal goal is to 'support sustainable economic growth and prosperity in the Asia-Pacific region'. It does this through supporting 'free and open trade and investment, promoting and accelerating regional economic integration, encouraging economic and technical cooperation, enhancing human security, and facilitating a favourable and sustainable business environment'. It has historically, and to the discomfort of some members, also occasionally broadened out to cover some security issues, particularly prior to 2005 when the East Asia Summit (EAS) was launched.[210]

The idea of APEC was first publicly broached by Prime Minister Bob Hawke of Australia, in a speech in South Korea in 1989. Later that year, 12 Asia-Pacific countries met in Australia to establish APEC, in part owing to fears of growing Japanese dominance.

Between 1989 and 1992, APEC met as an informal senior official and ministerial dialogue. In 1993 President Bill Clinton established the practice of an annual APEC Economic Leaders' Meeting.

Future trajectory: A number of disputes (South Korea/ Japan, Japan/China, China/Russia) were evident in the 2012 meeting. The goal of enhancing economic links also suffered a setback with the rate of growth in trade between members in 2012 declining sharply from 12% in December 2011 to 4.6% in May 2012.[211] The 2013 meeting was marred

[206] US Department of State, 'US Engagement in the 2013, ASEAN Regional Forum', 2 July 2012, www.state.gov/r/pa/prs/ps/2013/07/211467.htm.

[207] 'South China Sea tension tops Asean regional agenda', BBC News, 9 July 2012, www.bbc.co.uk/news/world-asia-18765094.

[208] Association of Southeast Asian Nations, 'Overview of ASEAN-US Dialogue Relations', www.asean.org/asean/external-relations/united-states/item/overview-of-asean-us-dialogue-relations; and Association of Southeast Asian Nations, 'Overview, ASEAN-Japan Dialogue Relations', http://www.asean.org/news/item/external-relations-japan-overview-of-asean-japan-relations.

[209] 'ASEAN Plus Three to seek expansion of economic ties amid territorial disputes', *Japan Times*, 20 November 2011, www.japantimes.co.jp/news/2012/11/20/national/asean-plus-three-to-seek-expansion-of-economic-ties-amid-territorial-disputes/#.UW1V9yKs16Z; 'China, S. Korea ministers skip ASEAN-plus-3 finance meeting', *Global Post*, 5 May 2013, http://www.globalpost.com/dispatch/news/kyodo-news-international/130503/china-s-korea-ministers-skip-asean-plus-3-finance-meet.

[210] Asia-Pacific Economic Cooperation, 'Mission Statement', www.apec.org/About-Us/About-APEC/Mission-Statement.aspx.

[211] Elaine Kurtenbach, 'APEC seeks growth boost despite politics, tensions', Yahoo Finance, 7 September 2012, http://finance.yahoo.com/news/apec-seeks-growth-boost-despite-politics-tensions-010527853--finance.html.

by President Obama's absence (owing to the US government shutdown) and continuing tensions over security issues.[212]

However, as the principal Asian economic group, it is attractive to several countries, in particular India. Despite this, APEC has decided to not accept any new members until 2015.[213] APEC formally started discussing the concept of a free trade area of the Asia-Pacific in 2006. However, the idea has been around since at least 1966 and considerable barriers to progress remain.

East Asia Summit (EAS)

Membership: Australia, Brunei, Cambodia, China, India, Indonesia, Japan, Laos, Malaysia, Burma (Myanmar), New Zealand, Philippines, Russia, Singapore, South Korea, Thailand, United States, Vietnam.

The EAS brings together leaders from the region annually for 'strategic dialogue and cooperation on key challenges facing the East Asian region'. It covers, among other issues, security topics and is today arguably the principal institution addressing these issues in the region; unlike many of the others (including for example, ASEAN) it has all the major regional powers as members.[214]

The launch of the EAS in 2005 was initially mooted by China and Malaysia with the intent of excluding other potential regional powers such as India, Australia and New Zealand. However, some of the other original members fought against what they perceived to be the inevitable imbalance that this would create and drove for their inclusion. In 2011 membership expanded to 18 countries when the United States and Russia joined. The European Union would very much like to become a member. EAS meetings are held after annual ASEAN leaders' meetings.

Future trajectory: Given that this grouping includes all the major regional powers, its meetings have at times been quite controversial. Tensions both between states (such as Cambodia and Thailand) and within states (in Thailand and Burma (Myanmar)) have risen to the surface on various occasions. The 2012 meeting ended badly following tense discussions between China and several other countries over maritime/territorial issues and the 2013 suffered from the non-attendance of President Obama (as mentioned above).[215]

While the problems at recent gatherings were cause for concern, there is still plenty of scope for cooperation and conflict management at future meetings on issues as varied as energy, disaster relief, health, maritime security and non-proliferation.

Trans-Pacific Partnership (TPP)

Membership: Australia, Brunei, Canada, Chile, Japan, Malaysia, New Zealand, Mexico, Peru, Singapore, United States, Vietnam.

The TPP is a proposed free trade agreement under negotiation between 12 countries bordering the Pacific. It comes out of the 2005 Trans-Pacific Strategic Economic Partnership Agreement (TPSEP or P4), which was a free trade agreement between Brunei, Chile, New Zealand and Singapore that aimed to further liberalize the economies of the Asia-Pacific region. In 2008, the United States, Chile, New Zealand and Singapore launched discussions to expand the TPP, which have since been joined by various countries, including Japan in 2013.[216]

Future trajectory: The initial hope had been to complete negotiations on the TTP by the end of 2013. However, in particular following Japanese Prime Minister Abe's decision to join the negotiations, this timeline seemed very ambitious. There remain a number of sensitive issues on the table, between many of the member states, over such issues as intellectual property rights, pharmaceuticals and agriculture.

Many believe the TPP to be the US counterpoint to the Chinese-led Regional Comprehensive Economic Partnership (RCEP) negotiations that include Australia, China, India, Japan, South Korea, New Zealand and all ASEAN members. The progress of each set of negotiations is watched by many in the region and can cause some tensions and potential competition.

There is discussion of other countries joining the agreement once it has been completed, including conceivably China (it would be extremely hard for China to sign up to some of the intended norms, however, not least regarding state-owned enterprises) and South Korea (which has expressed some interest in joining).

[212] Murray Hiebert, Noelan Arbis and Kyle Springer, 'The 2013 APEC Leaders' Meeting and East Asia Summit', CSIS, 11 October 2013, https://csis.org/publication/2013-apec-leaders-meeting-and-east-asia-summit.
[213] Chris Devonshire-Ellis, 'India Appeals for APEC Membership', Asia Briefing, 6 October 2013, www.asiabriefing.com/news/2013/10/india-appeals-apec-membership/.
[214] Australian Government, Department of Foreign Affairs and Trade, 'The East Asia Summit', www.dfat.gov.au/asean/eas/.
[215] Ben Bland and Geoff Dyer, 'Tensions run high as East Asia Summit ends', *Financial Times*, 20 November 2012, http://www.ft.com/cms/s/0/4a0efc1e-32f8-11e2-aabc-00144feabdc0.html?siteedition=uk#axzz2uVzsuPMX.
[216] Chris Daniels, 'First step to wider free trade', *New Zealand Herald*, 10 February 2008, www.nzherald.co.nz/business/news/article.cfm?c_id=3&objectid=10491556.

Other organizations

There are a vast number of other organizations of which some of the Asia-Pacific powers considered here are members. For example, the South Asian Association for Regional Cooperation (SAARC) includes India, and the Shanghai Cooperation Organization (SCO) includes China alongside Russia, Kazakhstan and others. There are also competing economic organizations including the Bay of Bengal Initiative for Multi-Sectoral Technical and Economic Cooperation (BIMSTEC), the RCEP and others. However, those listed above are the principal actors in the security arena.

CPSIA information can be obtained at www.ICGtesting.com
Printed in the USA
BVOW10s0845190315

392291BV00006B/6/P